RESTRUCTURING
THE GATT SYSTEM

RESTRUCTURING THE GATT SYSTEM

John H. Jackson

PUBLISHED IN NORTH AMERICA FOR

THE ROYAL INSTITUTE OF INTERNATIONAL AFFAIRS

COUNCIL ON FOREIGN RELATIONS PRESS
• NEW YORK •

Dedicated to the memory of

Jan Tumlir
1926–1985

Director of the GATT Secretariat
Economic Research and Analysis Unit,
and author of perceptive and thoughtful books and
articles about the GATT 'constitution'.

Jackson, John Howard, 1932–
    Restructuring the GATT system / by John H. Jackson.
      p.   cm.—(Chatham House Papers)
    "Published . . . for the Royal Institute of International Affairs."
    Includes bibliographical references.
    ISBN 0-087609-076-5 : $14.95
    1. General Agreement on Tariffs and Trade (Organization)
2. General Agreement on Tariffs and Trade (1947) 3. Uruguay Round
(1987–) 4. Tariff—Law and legislation. 5. Foreign trade
regulation. I. Royal Institute of International Affairs.
II. Title. III. Series: Chatham House papers (Unnumbered)
K4602.2 1990   89-71227
341.7'543—dc20   CIP

90 91 92 93 94 95 96 97 PB 10 9 8 7 6 5 4 3 2 1

CONTENTS

Contents

1

INTRODUCTION

The GATT – the General Agreement on Tariffs and Trade – is generally recognized as the principal international organization and rule system governing most of the world's international trade. Yet this organization is a curious institution, to say the least. The basic treaty comprising the GATT has never come into force, being applied through a 1947 'Protocol of Provisional Application'.[1] After 40 years of 'provisional application', one might think that the world was ready for something more than 'provisional'! In addition, at its origin, the GATT was not intended as an international organization. Yet today, as it actually operates, it clearly falls well within any reasonable definition of 'international organization'.

World economic developments have pushed the GATT into playing an even more central role during the past 20 years. Even ten years ago, very few people would have known about it or recognized its name; now it figures prominently on the front pages of the world's major newspapers.

The growing economic interdependence of the nations of the world needs no comment. Armed conflict and social unrest in the Middle East affect farmers in Iowa and France and motor vehicle workers in Michigan and Germany. Interest-rate decisions taken in Washington have a profound influence on the external debt of many developing countries, which in turn affects their ability to purchase goods made in industrial countries and to provide their citizenry with economic advancement. Environmental problems have obvious cross-border effects. More and more frequently, government leaders find their freedom of action circumscribed because of the impact of external economic factors on their national economies.

Although the world has been blessed with 40 years of relative freedom from armed conflict, there is still a fundamental concern about how best to guard against war. The relationship between economic trends and armed conflict has always been recognized, and hence the implementation of international economic policy has a potentially powerful influence on the fundamental goal of current international relations – the avoidance of armed conflict. Yet often economic affairs are left to technical specialists or ministries charged with more limited objectives, so that there is a continuing risk of forgetting the linkages just expressed.

Because of its strange and quirky beginnings, this central international trade institution, the GATT, suffers from a number of serious constitutional defects. Indeed, given the ever-accelerating pace of change in economic relations in the world, the faster flow of economic influences across national borders, and the increasing intricacy of these influences (which makes them difficult to interpret), many persons are beginning to question whether the existing international institutions, particularly the GATT, will be able to cope.

The GATT is part of a broader system – the Bretton Woods system, which includes the major monetary institutions (the IMF and the World Bank) as well as a number of other treaty instruments. This entire system needs to be examined, since the GATT is only one part of the whole. However, that task is beyond the scope of this short study.

The purpose of this study is to examine the institutional and 'constitutional' structure of GATT, in the context of a number of fundamental issues and problems facing the world's principal international trade regime, and to suggest possible revisions in that structure. The term constitutional is here taken to cover the basic treaty structure of the GATT, as well as a system of more than 180 additional treaties that are closely related to the GATT.[2] It is this larger network of treaty instruments that forms the 'constitution' of the world's trading system as we can observe it today. It is also this vast network that adds considerably to the difficulty of coming to grips with the institution. In the chapters that follow I shall draw extensively upon other works that I have published on the subject, while shaping the text to the particular questions that this study is designed to address.[3]

In September 1986 the 'GATT system' sponsored a ministerial meeting at Punta del Este in Uruguay, designed to launch a new round of trade negotiations in the context of GATT. This round, scheduled to last until 1990, is currently under way and is the eighth such round sponsored by GATT since its initiation in 1947 (including the original negotiation at which the GATT itself was formed). One of the explicit items for this negotiation, as manifested by the terms of the 'Punta del Este declaration', was the 'functioning of the GATT system', often shortened to 'FOGS'. As expressed in that document:

Negotiation shall aim to develop understandings and arrangements:

(i) to enhance the surveillance in the GATT to enable regular monitoring of trade policies and practices of contracting parties and their impact on the functioning of the multilateral trading system;

(ii) to improve the overall effectiveness and decision-making of the GATT as an institution, including, *inter alia*, through involvement of Ministers;

(iii) to increase the contribution of the GATT to achieving greater coherence in global economic policy-making through strengthening its relationship with other international organizations responsible for monetary and financial matters.

In addition, certain other clauses in the Punta del Este declaration are addressed to 'the constitution' of GATT. For example, one of the negotiating groups was set up to consider the dispute settlement procedures of the GATT, and its charge reads:

In order to ensure prompt and effective resolution of disputes to the benefit of all contracting parties, negotiations shall aim to improve and strengthen the rules and the procedures of the dispute settlement process, while recognizing the contribution that would be made by more effective and enforceable GATT rules and disciplines. Negotiations shall include the development of adequate arrangements for overseeing and monitoring of the procedures that would facilitate compliance with adopted recommendations.

Furthermore, the Punta del Este declaration (with the new Uruguay Round of negotiations) has explicitly undertaken to examine and develop some international discipline or rules for several subjects that are new or almost new to the GATT system. Among these are trade in services, certain trade-related aspects of intellectual property rights (TRIPs), and trade-related investment measures (TRIMs). These subjects, if they lead to significant negotiating results in the Uruguay Round, have the potential vastly to increase the areas of responsibility and jurisdiction of the GATT system.

During the seventh round of trade negotiations, the Tokyo Round (1973–9), the GATT negotiators were successful for the first time in addressing a number of perplexing non-tariff barriers that had been restraining and influencing international trade flows to an increasing extent. Earlier GATT rounds tended to focus primarily on tariff reductions. The result of the Tokyo Round itself has been greatly to increase, perhaps to triple, the activity and subject jurisdiction of the GATT system. With the possibility that the Uruguay Round will once again greatly enlarge that subject's scope, we can immediately see the potential for further constitutional strains on the rather weak framework of the GATT.

A number of questions immediately come to mind. How do special-subject treaty agreements under the auspices of GATT relate to the GATT treaty obligations themselves? How can the system cope with the complexity and possible inconsistency of rules of its various treaty instruments? How should the dispute settlement process be structured to accommodate such a vast field of subject-matter? Does the complexity and scope of the system itself impose undue strains on smaller governments and those with a relative lack of expertise, making it difficult to have adequate representation at the GATT headquarters in Geneva, and to conduct a broad-based multilateral economic diplomacy frequently ensnared in highly

technical and diverse economic issues? How can the nation participants keep the rules up to date, to cope with the rapidly changing
economic developments?

Finally, the GATT, which started with a 1947 Geneva negotiation
involving 23 countries, has now 97 'members',[4] and a growing list of
provisional members and countries seeking membership. How can
this frail constitutional structure cope with such an explosive
enlargement of its membership, particularly when the basic treaty
instrument is so scanty in its reference to the typical international
organization subjects which govern an international institution
(such as voting, rule-making structures, secretariat services, finance
and budget, privileges and immunities)?

The objectives of this study, as defined by the Royal Institute of
International Affairs, were not only to examine matters related to
the 'FOGS' and the dispute settlement negotiating groups of the
Uruguay Round, but also to explore a series of fundamental
questions about the nature of the GATT and the direction in which
it might evolve. Busy negotiators are often so preoccupied with the
very technical and intricate issues raised by powerful special interest
groups in the participating countries that they find it difficult to step
back from the immediate problems and think in broader terms.

There is no claim that this subject has a specially high priority in
negotiations in world affairs – many other issues of the Uruguay
Round are undoubtedly more important. Yet the 'institutional' or
'constitutional' issues can have a profound longer-term effect on
those other issues as well as on the GATT system generally.

In this study, therefore, we will be concerned with longer-term
issues, at the risk occasionally of appearing disengaged from the
current negotiation, and possibly even of appearing unrealistic or
too 'idealistic'. On the other hand, in addition to suggesting where
the longer-term future of GATT might lie, this study will look at
intermediate steps that could be taken, perhaps even in the course of
the Uruguay Round, to solve some special problems of the GATT
constitutional framework, or to nudge the GATT system helpfully
towards some longer-term and more fundamental solutions.

This study is not intended to go into the substantive trade policy
rules or problems of GATT. Issues such as subsidies, anti-dumping
rules, agriculture, quantitative restrictions, safeguards, etc., will be
addressed only in so far as they are related to some of the
constitutional and institutional questions which we intend to focus

on. Thus, we will not be concerned with what should be the shape of a rule regarding trade in services; on the other hand we will be very concerned with how the GATT context will handle the effectuation and the evolution of such rules.

PART I

The Defective Constitution

of GATT

2

THE HISTORY AND PERSPECTIVE OF GATT

2.1 The origins of GATT

The major initiatives leading towards the GATT were taken by the United States, during World War II, in cooperation with its allies, particularly Great Britain. There were two distinct strands of thought which influenced those countries during the war period.[1] One of these strands stemmed from the programme of trade agreements begun by the United States after the enactment of the 1934 Reciprocal Trade Agreements Act. With this act the US Congress (responding to the unfortunate 1930 Smoot Hawley Tariff Act) delegated to the US President power to enter into reciprocal agreements to lower tariffs, and under this authority, renewed from time to time, the US by 1945 had entered into 32 bilateral agreements reducing tariffs. Later versions of these agreements contained most of the substantive clauses subsequently found in GATT.

The second strand of thinking during the war period stemmed from the view that recent mistakes concerning economic policy were a major cause of the disasters that led to World War II. The Great Depression has been partly blamed for this war, as has the harsh reparations policy towards Germany.[2] Between the wars, and particularly after the damaging 1930 US Tariff Act, nations took many protectionistic measures, including quota restrictions, which choked international trade. Political leaders in the US and elsewhere made statements about the importance of establishing post-war economic institutions that would prevent these mistakes from happening again.

The Bretton Woods conference, held in 1944, was devoted to monetary and banking issues, and it established the charters of the IMF (International Monetary Fund) and the World Bank (International Bank for Reconstruction and Development), but it did not take up the problems of trade as such. The conference was held under the jurisdiction of ministries of finance, who were not responsible for trade. Nevertheless the 1944 conference is on record as recognizing the need for a comparable institution for trade, to complement the monetary institutions.[3]

The two strands of thinking about an organization for international trade began to merge in 1945. The US Congress then enacted the 1945 renewal of the reciprocal trade agreements legislation for a three-year period.[4] In December of that year, the US government invited a number of other nations to enter into negotiations to conclude a multilateral agreement for the mutual reduction of tariffs. In the same year, the United Nations was formed, and in February 1946 its subordinate body, ECOSOC, at its first meeting, adopted a resolution calling for a conference to draft a charter for an 'international trade organization'.[5] The United States at this time published a draft ITO charter and a preparatory committee was formed and met in October 1946 in London. The principal meeting was held in Geneva from April to November 1947, and was followed by a meeting to complete the ITO charter in Havana, Cuba, in 1948.

The history of the preparation of GATT is intertwined with the preparation of the ITO charter. The 1947 Geneva meeting was actually an elaborate conference in three major parts. One part was devoted to continuing the preparation of a charter for a major international trade institution, the ITO. A second part dealt with the negotiation of a multilateral agreement reciprocally to reduce tariffs. A third part concentrated on drafting the general clauses of obligations relating to the tariff obligations. These later two parts together would constitute the GATT.

The general clauses of the draft GATT imposed obligations on nations to refrain from a variety of trade-impeding measures. Many of these clauses had evolved in the US bilateral trade agreements, and were seen as necessary to protect the value of any tariff-reducing obligations.[6] The GATT, however, was not intended to be an organization. Indeed, US negotiators were criticized by committees

Table 1 The 'constitutions' of GATT and the IMF compared

	GATT (1947)	IMF (1944)
Origin	Conferences on trade organization and multilateral tariff negotiation (not intended to be organization)	Bretton Woods Conference (established as international organization)
US adherence	Executive action pursuant to ambiguous statutory delegations	Congressional action – Bretton Woods Agreements Act 1945 controls US participation
Structure	CONTRACTING PARTIES acting jointly Council (by resolution; no mention in treaty) Consultative Group of 18 (by resolution; no mention in treaty)	Board of Governors (provided in charter) Executive Directors (provided in charter)
	Executive Secretary (in treaty) Director-General (by resolution)	Managing Director (provided in charter)
Secretariat	None in Treaty; 'leased' from ICITO	Provided in charter
Voting	One country/one vote	Weighted
Amendments	Unanimous or $\frac{2}{3}$; $\frac{2}{3}$ for rest (only applies to countries which accept)	$\frac{3}{5}$ (up to 85% in some cases). Binds all members
Interpretation	Joint action? (Article XXV)	Binding procedure (Article XXIX)
Disputes	Articles XXII & XXIII, but procedures developed by practice	Article XXIX
Sanctions	Retaliatory suspension of obligations towards offending party	Explusion or limitation of rights to use Fund
Finance	Contributions	Self-supporting (fees)
Membership	97 (as of Sept. 1989)* Articles XXVI & XXXIII	149 (as of Sept. 1985) Terms set by Board

* 93 GATT members are also members of the IMF.
Note: There are marked differences between the general clauses of the GATT treaty and the charters of the IMF or the World Bank (or almost any major international organization). The GATT lacks many of the normal organizational clauses of an international organization, and has huge gaps in its procedures as well as substantial ambiguities in its minuscule organizational provisions.

of the US Congress in 1947 for tentatively agreeing to clauses which seemed to imply an organization. The US President and his negotiators recognized that an ITO charter would have to be submitted to Congress for approval. But from the US point of view, the GATT was being negotiated under the 1945 extension of the trade agreements authority. The Congressional committees pointed out that this 1945 Act did not authorize the President to enter into an agreement for an organization – it only authorized agreements to reduce tariffs and other restrictions on trade. So the US negotiators returned to Geneva and redrafted the general GATT clauses to avoid the suggestion of an organization. Thus multilateral decisions under GATT are taken by the 'CONTRACTING PARTIES acting jointly' and not by any 'organization'.[7]

The Geneva negotiators in 1947 thus pursued the goal of preparing a draft ITO charter (to be completed at Havana in 1948), and also negotiating elaborate schedules of tariff reductions appended to the general clauses of GATT. These schedules consisted of thousands of individual tariff commitments applied to all GATT members through the most-favoured nation (MFN) obligation.[8]

Since the GATT was designed to be merely a multilateral treaty, not an organization, it would be similar to the bilateral treaties which preceded it, but designed to operate under the umbrella of the ITO when that organization came into being. The general clauses of GATT were the same as those in the chapter of the draft ITO charter which was devoted to trading rules, and that in turn had been heavily influenced by clauses in bilateral trade treaties. After the ITO charter was completed, parallel GATT clauses would be revised to bring them into conformity with those of the ITO charter.[9]

The Havana Conference in 1948 completed the draft ITO charter, but the ITO never came into being, because the United States Congress failed to approve it. The US President submitted the Havana Charter (ITO draft) to the Congress in mid 1948, but after several years it became clear that the Congress would not approve the charter, and in 1951 the President announced that he would no longer seek approval.[10] The irony was that it was the US that had taken the principal initiative to develop the ITO charter in the first place.

How is it that the GATT as such has never come into force, and yet that it is known as the principal institution of international trade today? The answer technically lies in the Protocol of Provisional

Application, through which the GATT is applied as a treaty obligation under international law. This situation was a direct result of the history outlined above, but needs further explanation.

The GATT was completed by October 1947, before the ITO charter to which it was to be subordinated. Yet many negotiators felt that the GATT should be brought into force before the ITO, for several reasons. First, although the tariff concessions were still secret, the negotiators were aware that their content would begin to be known. World trade patterns could thus be seriously disrupted if a prolonged wait occurred before the tariff concessions came into force.[11]

Second, US negotiators were acting on the authority of the US trade legislation which had been renewed in 1945 and under which they would not need to submit the GATT to Congress. There was a strong motivation on the part of the US to bring the GATT into force before this act expired in mid 1948.[12] It was unlikely that this could be done if the participants in these events waited until after the 1948 Havana Conference and the completion of the ITO charter.

On the other hand there were several problems involved in the enforcement of GATT. Some could be handled by amending the GATT at a later date to make it conform with the results of the later Havana Conference. Some nations, however, had constitutional procedures under which they could not agree to parts of the GATT without submitting this agreement to their parliaments. Since they anticipated the need to submit the final draft of the ITO charter to their parliaments shortly afterwards, they preferred to take both agreements to their legislatures as a package.[13]

The solution agreed upon was the adoption of the 'Protocol of Provisional Application'. By this protocol eight nations agreed to apply the GATT 'provisionally on and after 1 January 1948', while the remaining 15 members would do so soon after. The protocol contained several other important clauses which resulted in changing the impact of the GATT itself.

The much more important impact of the PPA, however, is its manner of implementing GATT. Parts I and III of GATT are fully implemented without a PPA exception, but the PPA called for implementation of Part II 'to the fullest extent not inconsistent with existing legislation'. Part I of GATT contains the MFN and the tariff concession obligations, while Part III is mainly procedural. Part II (Articles III to XXIII) contains most of the major substantive obligations, including those relating to customs procedures, quotas, subsidies, anti-dumping duties, and national treatment. With regard to these important obligations, each GATT Contracting Party was entitled to 'grandfather rights' for any provision of its legislation existing when it became a party, and which was inconsistent with a GATT Part II obligation.

These 'grandfather rights', or the 'existing legislation' exception of the PPA, solved for most countries the problem of executive authority to agree to GATT. This exception allowed most governments which would otherwise have needed to submit the GATT for legislative approval to approve the PPA by executive or administrative authority without going to the legislature. Obviously it was contemplated that after the ITO charter was ready to submit to legislatures, the GATT would also be submitted for definitive application. In the meantime, GATT Contracting Parties could deviate from those GATT Part II obligations to which they could not adhere without legislative authority. They must accept fully the MFN obligation of Article I of GATT and the tariff cuts of Article II incorporating the tariff schedules, but in most cases the executives had authority to do this. Governments which later joined the GATT did so on treaty terms which incorporated the same 'existing legislation' exception.

Although there have subsequently been attempts to obtain definitive application of the GATT, none has succeeded.[14] Thus even today grandfather rights are invoked to justify certain national actions regarding international trade.[15] This legal context was an important part of the US bargaining position in the Tokyo Round negotiation of a countervailing duty code,[16] since the US countervailing duty law which predated GATT did not require an injury test. Thus, the US agreement to extend the injury test to trade from other countries became the quid pro quo for those countries accepting greater international disciplines on the use of subsidies for goods which were exported.

Many of the grandfather rights have, however, become extinct. Any new legislation does not qualify for this PPA exception, and gradually some of the old provisions have passed out of existence, or have for other reasons become non-operative or been superseded.[17] For example, all EEC laws came into existence after GATT, and so received no grandfathering, and since the EEC took over competence on external trade from member states, it is likely that most grandfathered provisions of EC members were lost. In other cases, new legislation superseded old rules, and the grandfather right was lost. Indeed, there is some indication that very few grandfathered rules persist. The US still claims a few, including measures relating to agricultural products (to be distinguished from measures covered in US law by a 1955 agriculture GATT waiver, which do not depend on the PPA). One possible significant US grandfather right is still the lack of injury test in countervailing duty cases involving countries which have not accepted the subsidy obligations of the Tokyo Round code. This situation, however, is clouded by the arguments that the GATT MFN clause (never subject to grandfather rights) requires the US in any case to relinquish its 'hold-out' position on the countervailing injury test.

2.2 GATT substitutes for the ITO

Since the ITO did not come into being, a major gap was left in the fabric intended for post-World War II international economic institutions – the Bretton Woods system. It was only natural that that institution which did exist – the GATT – would find its role changing dramatically as nations began to regard it as a forum to handle an increasing number of problems of their trading relationships. More countries became Contracting Parties. Because of the fiction that GATT was not an organization, there was considerable reluctance at first to delegate any activity even to a committee. Gradually that reluctance faded, and soon there was even an 'intersessional committee'[18] which met between sessions of the Contracting Parties.

No secretariat existed for the GATT. After Havana, however, an 'Interim Commission for the ITO' (ICITO) was set up, in the typical pattern of preparing the way for a new international organization. A small staff was assembled to prepare the ground for the ITO, and this staff[19] serviced the needs of the GATT. As years passed and it became clear that the ITO was never to come into being, this staff found that all of its time was devoted to the GATT, and it became *de facto* the GATT secretariat. (Technically it was a sort of leased group, whereby the GATT reimbursed the ICITO for the costs of the secretariat.)

In the early 1950s the GATT CPs decided to review the GATT and amend it for its developing role as the central international institution for trade. The CPs' ninth regular session, scheduled for 1954–5, was designated as a 'review session', and at this exceptionally long session extensive protocols were prepared to amend the GATT: one for those parts of GATT requiring unanimity to amend; another for those requiring only two-thirds acceptance. Ultimately the latter protocol came into effect, amending portions of Part II of GATT, but the protocol requiring unanimity never came into force and was withdrawn in 1967.[20]

The 1955 review session also drafted a new organizational protocol. Under this protocol an 'Organization for Trade Cooperation' (OTC) was to be established to provide the institutional framework for the developing organizational role of GATT. This short treaty agreement was much less elaborate than the ITO, but even it failed to get the approval of the US Congress, so the OTC too was stillborn.[21] The last formal amendment to the GATT was a 1965 protocol to add Part IV, dealing with problems of developing countries.[22]

Thus the GATT has limped along for over 40 years with almost no basic 'constitution' designed to regulate its organizational activities and procedures. Even so, by any fair definition it must be today deemed an international organization and has evolved (through experimentation and trial and error) some fairly elaborate procedures for conducting its business. That it could do so with the flawed basic documents on which it had to build is a tribute to the pragmatism and ingenuity of many of its leaders over the years. It is certainly clear that the GATT has been much more successful than one could fairly predict in 1951 when the ITO idea died. The GATT has an admirable record of tariff rate reductions, at least regarding industrial products imported by industrial countries. Of course, as tariffs were lowered, the attention of domestic producer interests turned to other devices to eliminate competition from imports. These 'non-tariff measures' are the crucial terrain of trade policy today, and inventories can easily list thousands of NTMs. Regarding these, the GATT record is far less admirable. The proliferation of so-called 'grey-area measures' whose legality is open to question has been troublesome. The loopholes and ambiguities of GATT, coupled with its inability to adjust to the new 'protectionist technologies', such as voluntary restraint measures, are what must concern anyone trying to appraise GATT's ability to discipline nations in the interests of evolving a successful trade policy. The far-reaching grey-area measures on textiles, cars, steel, and now on computer parts, are all problematic in this regard.

In addition, the GATT has heretofore been unable effectively to regulate national government trade measures on agriculture products. (The 1955 waiver given to the US didn't help.) Furthermore, a number of developing countries have been able to take advantage of various GATT exceptions to maintain very protectionist regulations. Likewise the GATT has failed to develop a satisfactory mechanism for disciplining state-trading activities.

Many of these problems are related to the constitutional defects of GATT, although they are by no means solely caused by them.

3

THE GATT
'CONSTITUTION'

3.1 GATT as an organization; membership and institutional measures

Despite the original intention of the draughtsmen that GATT was not to be an international organization, history forced it to assume that role. Effectively GATT became an organization for consultation, negotiation, and the application of rules regarding international trade. In this chapter we survey briefly some of these 'organizational' aspects of the GATT.

(a) *Who belongs to GATT*

Since in theory GATT is not an 'organization', it does not have 'members'; the terminology used in the agreement itself is 'contracting party', to emphasize this theory. Yet one can fairly speak of 'membership', in the light of its subsequent evolution.

Apart from being original GATT Contracting Parties, nations become GATT CPs by one of two methods. The normal method of accession is governed by Article XXXIII of GATT and requires a two-thirds vote of approval by the existing Contracting Parties. The applicant nation must negotiate tariff or other concessions which existing GATT CPs deem adequate to fulfil 'reciprocity' to existing GATT concessions. It would be unfair to let a nation enter GATT and receive the advantage of over 40 years of various trade concessions and obligations which the existing CPs had accepted, unless the new nation committed itself to equivalent obligations. This is sometimes referred to as negotiating the 'ticket of admission'.

A second path to GATT 'membership' is Article XXVI, paragraph 5(c), which provides that if a parent country has accepted the GATT in respect of a dependent customs territory (such as a colony), and that customs territory later becomes independent, such territory can become a GATT Contracting Party merely upon sponsorship by the parent country. To date, over 30 newly independent nations have entered GATT membership by this route. The advantage to those nations is that they need not negotiate a 'ticket of admission'. The GATT is deemed to apply to these newly independent sponsored nations to the same extent that it applied to their territories before independence. If the parent country had a sub-portion of its tariff schedule which applied to a territory, then that becomes the GATT schedule for the new Contracting Party. Often this would have only a few tariff obligations. If there were no such tariff schedule portion of the parent, however, then the new GATT party has the great privilege of belonging to GATT without obligations of any tariff concessions.[1]

Subsequently some of these Contracting Parties have added to their schedules by negotiation, but the provisions of Article XXXVI (8) of GATT (which specify that developing countries should not be obliged to furnish reciprocal concessions in tariff or trade negotiations) have influenced industrial countries to tolerate very short schedules of concessions from developing countries, even though these countries all benefit from the industrial country concessions by virtue of the MFN clause.

An important provision in Article XXXV affects the GATT obligations from and to a new 'member'. This article, introduced in the original 1947 GATT draft when the voting requirement for new members was reduced from unanimity to two-thirds, allows either a prior CP or a new CP to 'opt out' of a GATT relationship with the other at one time only – when the new CP enters GATT.[2] This was used extensively against Japan when it became a member, and has been used by other countries for a variety of reasons. Often the reason for objecting to a GATT relationship is political, such as India's original 1948 invocation of Article XXXV against South Africa.[3] This 'opt-out' clause has been carried into several of the 1979 Tokyo Round 'codes'.[4]

Membership of GATT is not limited to 'sovereign nations'. The agreement allows a 'separate customs territory possessing full autonomy in the conduct of its external commercial relations and of other matters provided for in this Agreement' to become a Contracting Party.[5] The most notable recent example of this is the case of Hong Kong.

Several interesting 'membership' questions are raised by the GATT. One is the status of the European Community. It is possible to argue that the EC is a 'separate customs territory possessing full autonomy' over GATT matters so that it could itself become a Contracting Party. Yet it has not taken steps to do so. All EC member states are GATT CPs, but the Treaty of Rome allocates competence over member states' external trade relations to the EC institutions. The EC Commission has a mission at GATT and asserts the sole right to speak for the member states at GATT on trade matters. There have been occasional instances, however, when some tension on this question arose between the EC Commission representatives and the member states. In addition, in several instances the Commission did not have competence regarding a matter discussed in GATT, so the member states spoke and acted for themselves. When voting occurs (and this is rare) each member state casts its vote as a Contracting Party (usually coordinated by the EC), and thus the EC effectively has 12 votes.[6]

China was one of the original Contracting Parties of GATT, but arguably withdrew from GATT in 1950 (a matter which is disputed because the withdrawal communication came from Taiwan).[7] China joined the GATT Multi-Fibre Agreement in 1984, became an observer to GATT in that same year,[8] and is currently negotiating for 'resumption' of its seat.

The case of Hong Kong also raises interesting questions of GATT 'membership'. For many years Hong Kong has participated in GATT as a colony of the United Kingdom.[9] In April 1986 Hong Kong was accepted by GATT as a full Contracting Party, after declaration of the UK under Article XXVI. Thus, to become a 'member', it was necessary to establish that Hong Kong was an independent customs territory with full autonomy over its external trade relations. As is well known, the UK possession of Hong Kong and adjacent territories is scheduled to end in 1997 under an agreement between the UK and the People's Republic of China. Assurances were received from the People's Republic of China that

Hong Kong's status would remain sufficiently independent to fulfil the GATT Article XXVI requirement, before Hong Kong was accepted as a Contracting Party to GATT.[10] Some students of China conjecture that this GATT requirement, coupled with the implicit risk of withdrawal of GATT 'membership', may be one of the more effective checks on temptations to depart from agreements regarding Hong Kong.

(b) The CPs acting jointly

For an agreement which is not supposed to be an 'organization' the GATT contains some clauses which appear to sanction a very broad exercise of authority. The principal body of GATT is the 'CON-TRACTING PARTIES' (specified in capital letters in the agreement when they are to 'act jointly'). A number of GATT clauses call for joint action, but Article XXV of the agreement gives general authority to the CPs to meet 'from time to time for the purpose of giving effect to those provisions of this Agreement which involve joint action and, generally, with a view to facilitating the operation and furthering the objectives of this Agreement'. Each CP gets one vote, and unless otherwise specified, a majority of votes cast controls an issue.

The terms of Article XXV could potentially provide very broad CP authority, though in practice this has not been widely used. Many governments (including the US) could have some serious constitutional problems if the CPs enforced Article XXV to its limit.

The CONTRACTING PARTIES carry out their business today with an elaborate group of committees, working parties, panels, and other bodies.[11] The most significant sub-body of the CPs is the 'Council', which was set up by resolution of the CONTRACTING PARTIES in 1960. This group consists of representatives of all GATT Contracting Parties who wish to assume the responsibility of such membership (now numbering approximately 74) and meets almost monthly.[12] Partly because of the formation of this group, but also because diplomacy has increasingly become a process of referring to national capitals for instructions and even voting by telex or fax, the sessions of the CONTRACTING PARTIES as such have been reduced to annual meetings which last only a few days. Day-to-day GATT business is carried on by the Council, supervising the many other bodies of GATT.

Now that GATT has 97 or more nations as Contracting Parties, it is no longer the cosy group of founder members. This has made effective operation more difficult. There is a trend for major GATT trading countries to take their business elsewhere – to annual summit meetings, for example, or to other private meetings of trade ministers.[13] Even though GATT may try to work by consensus, voting will often work against the interests of the most powerful CPs. For these various reasons, it has sometimes been suggested that GATT needs some sort of high-level committee which can act more like an executive, and which would reflect more accurately the real-power relations in the organization. The weighted voting technique of the IMF and the World Bank is not deemed a realistic option, but a possible framework might comprise a small group of nations which included the most powerful trading entities as well as representatives of major categories of other CPs. In 1975, during the Tokyo Round negotiations, a 'Consultative Group of 18' was set up, partly with these considerations in mind. It has not played a powerful role, however.[14] A question to be discussed therefore is what type of body could be created for the GATT, to help overcome some of its institutional problems. The 1955 'OTC' agreement discussed later addressed this question.[15]

For each major negotiating round in GATT, there has been formed a 'trade negotiations committee' (TNC). For the Uruguay Round the supervising structure became more complex because of some objections to GATT negotiations on services trade. The compromise reached provides for a typical negotiating group (called the GNG, Group on Negotiations of Goods) for trade negotiations on goods, but a separate supervising group for services (called the GNS, Group of Negotiations on Services). Some argue that the services group is not a GATT entity. Over both, however, is a broader supervising mechanism,[16] the TNC.

(c) Voting and consensus

The CONTRACTING PARTIES acting jointly are governed by majority vote on many matters; however, in much GATT business there is a decided preference for 'consensus' approaches. There is in fact some fear of voting, possibly with good reason. The voting structure, like that of so many international organizations today, bears little resemblance to the real power relations of the participants. The practice in GATT generally seeks to avoid formal voting except in the case of waivers, membership, and treaty amendments.

Nevertheless, the legal structure of potential voting still has a great influence on any organization, no matter how hard the organization tries to avoid voting. Consensus approaches often involve negotiating to resolve differences, but such negotiation is in the context of the participants' knowledge of the likely outcome if the negotiation breaks down. This can be complex and subtle. The outcome may be a vote, in which case the voting structure will in fact influence the negotiations towards a consensus. On the other hand, voting for an unrealistic proposition is likely to lead one or more powerful participants to ignore the vote result. This too becomes one of the constraints in a negotiation, at least where the negotiators are responsible and reasonably realistic.

A consensus approach has other problems. Strictly applied, it gives every country a veto and thus reduces any potential initiative to the least common denominator. If not strictly applied, there will often be deference to the real 'power structure' participants and this may in fact give the most powerful of the group a larger share of the power than policy or equity might dictate. During the Tokyo Round, the actual negotiation often began with major decisions being made by only the United States, the European Communities, and Japan. A few countries, such as Canada, might elbow their way into these discussions, but even then the vast majority of the Contracting Parties and other negotiating nations might be excluded from real influence on the drafting of a proposed agreement until near the end of the process, at which time it was difficult to get changes made.[17] Negotiators in the Uruguay Round are trying to avoid this situation.

Likewise, the voting consensus question has posed great problems for the GATT dispute settlement procedure, rendering it difficult if not impossible to obtain Council approval of a panel report in a dispute, when the nation dissatisfied with the outcome of such report refuses to go along with a 'consensus' for Council approval.[18]

A similar problem exists for many of the 'code' agreements which resulted from the Tokyo Round. The institutional clauses are even more ambiguous than GATT, often not specifying voting arrangements at all.[19] In such a case 'consensus' was supposed to be the approach used, but if this breaks down (as is more likely as more nations join the various codes), then general international customary practice will almost inevitably lead to the interpretation that 'one nation, one vote' with majority rule will prevail.

Here is an outline of the characteristics of GATT membership, to illustrate various voting or other influence possibilities (as of September 1989):

Contracting Parties

Total number of CPs = 97

Of which:
Industrial = 25
(EC member states, 12)

Advanced developing = 9
Developing = 57
Non-market economies = 6

The total of EC member states plus EFTA countries plus GATT members associated with the EC in the Lomé Convention is at least 54, which could be a formidable bloc, although no particular evidence of EC large bloc voting (beyond the member states) can be detected.

Obviously the Advanced Developing and the Developing Countries comprise more than a two-thirds vote of the GATT, opening the possibility of some waivers that could displease the industrial countries. This also imposes constraints on the possibility of amending the agreement.

The overall experience and current practice of these voting institutions in GATT and the various GATT associated codes, however, suggests more potential for paralysis than for any voting abuses.

(d) Amending the GATT
In the light of the discussion above, the problems of amending the GATT become clearer. Amendments to Articles I, II, and XXIX require unanimous acceptance. Amending the remainder of GATT requires two-thirds acceptance of all Contracting Parties, but such an amendment is binding on only those CPs which accept it (a potentially messy arrangement).[20]

In recent years it has often been considered impractical to amend the GATT general clauses. Thus it was perceived to be too difficult to embody the non-tariff measure results of the Tokyo Round negotiation into amendments to the GATT. Getting over 90 parliaments to accept the results would probably have been too time-consuming, and besides such an approach would effectively have given much more negotiating power to the majority bloc of developing countries.

On the other hand, the development of 'side codes' or stand-alone ancillary special-subject treaties to enlarge and elaborate the GATT rules poses some technical legal and administrative difficulties. In 1980 I wrote about some of these difficulties in the following terms:

> The interrelationships between the various Codes and the GATT will become increasingly complex. Such complexity, in turn, will make it harder for the general public to understand the GATT–MTN system, perhaps resulting in less public support for that system over time. The complexity will hurt those countries that cannot devote additional governmental expertise to GATT representation problems. In addition, such complexity inevitably will give rise to a variety of legal disputes among GATT parties. Finally, it will contribute to the belief that the richer nations can control and can manipulate the GATT system for their own advantage.

> The most striking characteristic [of the Tokyo Round results] is the balkanization or fragmentation of dispute settlement under the various Agreements.[21]

One of the questions raised by side codes, which purport to bind only those nations which separately accept them, is the relationship of those codes to the obligations of GATT itself. We come back to this question in the next section.

At least in earlier phases of the Uruguay Round there is some suggestion that an attempt might be made to embody negotiating results in actual amendments to the GATT. It remains to be seen how realistic this approach might be. The delay factor alone counsels against relying too heavily on the amending power. On the other hand, it might be possible to combine a 'side code' approach with an amending approach. The 'code' could come into force for its signatories very easily, while obliging signatories to accept a GATT amendment. When enough acceptances had been received, the amendment would come into force and supersede the 'code'.

Another possibility would be to have one very large package which all negotiating countries must accept (without picking and choosing). This would facilitate some trade-offs, but might make others more difficult. Amendments could be part of this large package.

In appraising the potential for amending the GATT, even with a two-thirds acceptance, it should be noted that only 74% of the CPs are interested enough in GATT to become Council members.[22] Furthermore, the *most* acceptances obtained by a Tokyo Round 'code' treaty agreement has been 37 – not even close to 50% of the GATT membership!

3.2 GATT as a network of treaty agreements

The 'GATT System' is not just one treaty instrument, but actually a large cluster of treaties – more than 180,[23] including some agreements which amend the GATT, others which admit new members, some which change and add to the tariff schedule, and still others which govern certain special subjects (sometimes not entirely consistently with the GATT original treaty!). Many of these have been added to GATT during its seven completed rounds of trade negotiations. The most complex such round, and the one which added the most 'substantive' treaty obligations, was the seventh.

This last completed round of negotiation occurred from 1973 to 1979, and was called the Tokyo Round, or sometimes the 'MTN' (meaning 'multilateral trade negotiations'). In this round non-tariff measures were addressed extensively for the first time. Except for the original drafting of the GATT itself, the MTN results may well be the most far-reaching and substantively important product of the seven major trade rounds (see Table 2). The MTN results included, in addition to tariff-reduction protocols, nine special agreements and four 'understandings', dealing with subjects as follows:

Agreements on:
(1) Technical Barriers to Trade ('TECH')
(2) Government Procurement ('PROC')

(3)   Interpretation and Application of Articles VI, XVI, and XXIII (Subsidies) ('SUBS')
(4)   Arrangement regarding Bovine Meat ('MEAT')
(5)   International Dairy Arrangement ('DAIRY')
(6)   Implementation of Article VII (Custom Valuation) ('VAL')
(7)   Import Licensing Procedures ('LIC')
(8)   Trade in Civil Aircraft ('AIR')
(9)   Implementation of Article VI (Anti-Dumping Duties) ('AD')

Understandings on:

(1)   Differential and More Favourable Treatment, Reciprocity and Fuller Participation of Developing Countries
(2)   Declaration on Trade Measures Taken for Balance-of-Payments Purposes
(3)   Safeguard Action for Development Purposes
(4)   Understanding Regarding Notification, Consultation, Dispute Settlement and Surveillance.[24]

The overall impact of these results was substantially to broaden the scope of coverage of the GATT system.[25]

The legal status of these various agreements and understandings, however, is not always clear. The nine agreements are drafted as 'stand-alone' treaties, each with signatory clauses, and in most cases with institutional measures which include a committee of signatories with certain powers, and a dispute settlement mechanism (part of the 'Balkanization' mentioned earlier). Of these agreements, seven have sufficiently precise obligations to be called 'codes'. The others tend to confine their terms to the development of consultation mechanisms, statements of objectives, and only a few weak provisions which actually provide binding obligations. In one case, an agreement has been so problematic that the United States and some other signatories have formally withdrawn from it.[26]

The understandings have a much more ambiguous status. These instruments mostly express goals or very general obligations, or (in the case of dispute settlement) describe procedures which arguably were already followed. These are not signed as independent agreements. The CONTRACTING PARTIES in November 1979 adopted these understandings.[27] The implication of some of the provisions in these understandings is such as to suggest a 'waiver' from other GATT obligations,[28] while other provisions elaborate procedures in the

Table 2 Tokyo Round Agreement acceptances (as of 1 October 1989)

	TECH	PROC	SUBS	MEAT	DAIRY	VAL	LIC	AIR	AD
Acceptances									
EC member states[a]	0	11	11	11	12	10	11	0	11
Total accepted CPs[b]	35	23	34	32	26	39	37	19	35
Developed CPs[b]	21	11	13	11	8	14	13	17	12
Adv. developing	6	1	4	3	1	4	3	1	4
Less developed	4	0	6	3	2	4	5	0	3
Non-market	4	0	0	4	3	4	5	1	5
Non-GATT	2	0	0	4	1	1	0	0	0
Signed only[c] or Prov.	2	0	1	1	0	1	1	2	0
Observer[d]	28	33	30	17	20	24	28	18	27
Total participating	66	56	65	51	46	65	66	39	62

Source: GATT L/6453 and additions.
[a]EC member states bound by EC acceptances, though not having separately accepted.
[b]EC not counted as a CP.
[c]Signed, but ratification procedures not completed.
[d]Some observers not GATT CPs.

manner in which a 'decision' under GATT Article XXV might do. The understanding regarding dispute settlement has been extremely important, since the GATT treaty provisions on this subject are so scanty. This understanding (which, however, has a number of ambiguities) has provided a reasonably definitive account of the practice which had developed over the decades of GATT activity.

As stand-alone treaties, the codes bind only those nations which sign and ratify them. A number of questions can then be raised about the legal relationship of these codes to the GATT itself. First, in theory, GATT parties which do not sign the agreements are not bound by them, and no provision of a code can alter their GATT rights. Since the GATT obligations include the most-favoured-nation clause, however, if a code provides treatment for the trade of any other code signatory which is more favourable than that provided in GATT, such treatment is arguably required to benefit a GATT member which has not signed the code. The GATT CON-TRACTING PARTIES in November 1979 adopted a decision[29] which takes this position. However, some codes may not fall within the terms of the GATT MFN clause, for example, Government Procurement.

Some of the 'codes' have titles which relate them to the GATT, such as the 'Agreement on Implementation of Article VI', and another on 'Interpretation and Application of' several GATT Articles. Again, non-signatories can argue that they are in no way bound by such codes. However, if these codes can be deemed to be 'practice' of the GATT Contracting Parties, they could themselves be evidence of evolving interpretation of the GATT language itself. This could be especially true if further practice in GATT develops, without protest from non-signatories of the codes, which follows a code interpretation. In these ways GATT parties who have not signed a code may find that they effectively become bound by code terms which 'interpret' the GATT.[30]

One issue already posed is the question of membership in some of the codes, when a customs territory becomes a Contracting Party by 'mother country' sponsorship.[31] In such a case, does the new CP also automatically become a member of such codes which the sponsoring parent country had signed?[32] The fact that the GATT secretariat services the codes and their committees also raises questions about the relationship. Are all GATT members entitled at least to be observers in a code committee of signatories, even if they do not themselves sign the code? So far the code committees have all taken the position that they are entitled to decide which governments may be observers and attend meetings of their code. Most have, however, always accepted requests from other GATT members to be observers. On the other hand, the code committees have reserved the right to meet occasionally without observers, and to limit the participation of non-signatories. It should be noted, incidentally, that certain nations which are not GATT members are allowed to become signatories to some codes.[33]

Finally it should be recalled that many of the codes have independent dispute settlement mechanisms.[34] This raises the issue of whether a particular dispute should be brought according to the general GATT procedure, or under the separate code procedure (or both), and disputes about this have occurred. It also has the potential of giving rise to questions about what happens when an interpretation of a code by a code dispute panel differs from an interpretation of a similar GATT issue by a GATT panel.

Clearly some thought is needed about the relationship of special code-type agreements to the GATT, and the appropriate role in such a code of GATT CPs which do not sign the code. Perhaps, at least, all GATT members should be automatically designated observers and have the right to be kept informed about code activity.

3.3 National legal systems and GATT

The link between national and international rules is an essential ingredient of any international institution, and this is particularly true of the GATT system. The interplay of GATT and a number of national constitutions and laws is extremely important to the operation and understanding of that system. This, of course, adds considerable (though unavoidable) complexity to the system. In some sense a complete analysis of this facet of the institution would require examination of 97 (or more) national constitutional systems. Since that would be impractical, this monograph will consider the links between national laws of the US, Japan, and the EC on the one hand, and the GATT system on the other.

Some countries, including the United States, make a distinction between international law and domestic law. This distinction concerns whether an international treaty will be treated by courts and government agencies as part of the domestic law of a country, similar to statute law. Some countries, notably the United Kingdom, are considered 'dualist' and treaties are not part of the domestic law. For domestic law implementation of a treaty to occur, the Parliament must enact a statute, or there must be promulgated some other legal instrument (such as an executive decree or regulation). Other countries have legal systems which tend to incorporate international agreements into domestic law without the intervention of further governmental acts.[35] These are often termed 'monist' systems. The United States falls in between. International agreements can sometimes be deemed to apply automatically as 'statute-like' law in domestic US courts.

It must be recognized that a treaty norm may well be valid and binding for international law purposes, but not be part of a domestic law system. This gives rise to the possibility that the domestic law which prevails in specific cases is inconsistent with the international law treaty norm. In such a case the country concerned may be in violation of its international law obligations, although its domestic law will be valid in its own government institutions, including its courts. These issues can be very significant in connection with, for example, the GATT, and the various 'side codes'. Furthermore the legal treatment of these trade agreements may differ from country to country, giving rise to perceptions of unfairness or lack of reciprocity.[36]

The United States

There is a great deal of confusion about US law relating to domestic application of international agreements, and this confusion is reflected in the court opinions and in the secondary literature.[37]

It has sometimes been said that the GATT is not a valid binding obligation on the United States, but this is clearly wrong.[38] In addition, for certain technical reasons most of the GATT is part of domestic US law, although the Tokyo Round agreements are not. The rules of these latter agreements (but not the agreements themselves) are incorporated into US law by the 1979 Statute which authorized the US President to accept them, but the Congress explicitly denied these agreements 'self-executing' status.

The GATT agreement itself might logically, under US law, be directly applicable or 'self-executing'. However, the GATT is only applied by the Protocol of Provisional Application, and this Protocol's wording appears to prevent 'self-execution'. This does not cause many problems because all except Part IV of GATT has been 'proclaimed' by the President pursuant to statutory authority, and has thus become 'statute-like law' in the US. Nevertheless, the US 'later in time' rule means that later federal statutes and regulations can override the GATT in domestic US law (but not in international law).

The US constitutional system has had a most profound influence on the GATT's origin and development. The founding fathers who wrote the United States Constitution in the 1780s distrusted government and concentrations of power. Consequently, they built into the Constitution the concept of distributing power among three principal branches of the federal government (the Presidency or executive branch, the Congress, and the courts), and between the federal government and the state governments. They thus set up a system of checks and balances, which would prevent any one branch from becoming too powerful. Among the results of this structure is a constant tension between the Congress and the executive branch.

Even though the Congress has lately reasserted its powers in connection with foreign affairs, the presidential powers are formidable, and still dominant. The President has authority to negotiate international agreements and consequently he can enter into some (few) executive agreements on his own constitutional authority. More significantly, however, over the years the Congress has delegated to the President a wide variety of powers relating to international affairs. Since the President is the chief negotiator in international affairs, he can sometimes effectively exercise great power.

The role of the Congress in trade policy is extremely important, and to some, very troublesome. The authority of the US executive branch in this subject derives principally from enactments of the Congress. A number of these are enactments which the executive has sought from Congress. When the Congress grants authority in this area, however, it usually extracts some price, requiring certain procedural or judicial restraints on executive action, or mandating certain trade policy activity which may have important consequences. Often such authority is extended for a limited time and must be renewed periodically.

Federal courts in the United States, in exercising their constitutional role of mediating the division of powers within the US government, have played a relatively cautious role. With respect to foreign affairs, they seem to have deferred extensively to the President.[39] This deference has carried over into some but not all international economic affairs. On certain trade matters, however, the courts have not always deferred, reviewing matters of anti-dumping and countervailing duty questions in great detail.

The United States is a federal system, and the Constitution reserves certain powers to the states. However, with regard to international economic matters, there appears today to be no significant constitutional limitation on the powers of the federal government through state powers. Thus either a valid international agreement which has direct application, or any otherwise valid federal statute or regulation regarding foreign economic affairs, will be likely to prevail over inconsistent state law.[40]

The European Communities

The starting-point for understanding the broad outlines of the EC 'constitution' is an examination of the five entities or groups which play the key constitutional roles in the EC: the Commission, the

Council of Ministers, the Court of Justice, the European Parliament, and finally the member states. Each of these plays a distinct role, which is constantly evolving in a sort of dance of power contests and struggles, not unlike that which the United States experiences with its 'separation of powers' problems between the executive branch and Congress.

One of the very interesting features of the EC is the degree to which the EC as a whole is heavily influenced by legal structures and concepts. Even though many of the largest member states have constitutional structures that do not permit judicial review of parliamentary action, the EC as a collectivity effectively does have a judicial review system, with its Court playing a central role. Likewise, although an unwritten constitution is a feature of one of the largest member states, the EC to which it belongs has an elaborate written constitution (the 1957 Treaty of Rome and related treaties[41]) which is subject to definitive interpretation by the Court.

The Commission is the EC's closest counterpart to the executives of member states. The Council of Ministers, on the other hand, is composed of representatives of each of the member states, who sit as representatives, and not as civil servants or executives. The Council reviews and controls the actions of the Commission, except to the extent that the foundation treaties delegate direct responsibility to the Commission, or to the extent that the Council itself has so delegated. The legislative process most often consists of an interaction between the Commission and the Council, whereby the Commission proposes, and the Council must approve of a proposal before it becomes law.

The European Court of Justice (ECJ) is a central and significant part of the EC institutional structure, and has evolved into rather a strong constitutional court for the EC. Its influence is felt daily in the other EC institutions, and officials often find their discourse centred on questions about how the Court might react to this or that proposal.

A key question for the international trading system is the treaty-making authority of the EC, and the method by which the EC can participate in organizations such as GATT. The Treaty of Rome provides that in matters relating to the conduct of commercial policy the Community is to have exclusive competence.[42] The negotiation of commercial agreements with third countries is undertaken by the Commission alone, and concluded by the Council on behalf of the Community by a qualified majority. Relationships with interna-

33

tional organizations such as GATT are dealt with in specific Articles.[43] Another significant question is the effect on domestic law of international agreements accepted by the EC institutions. Can these become a direct part of the jurisprudence of the EC, both at the EC level (e.g. before the Court in an EC matter), and at the member state level (e.g. as directly applicable before member state domestic courts)? The answer appears to depend on a combination of factors, but it is not at all clear how far this principle will be extended to give EC international agreements the effect of domestic law.[44] In particular, the ECJ has ruled that some GATT clauses do not have direct effect, although this decision has been criticized and the Court's thinking on this may change.

Japan
The government of Japan differs considerably from those of the US and the EC. Japan has essentially a parliamentary form of government, and thus its executive is headed by a number of ministers, including the prime minister, who are almost always members of Parliament belonging to the party which has the parliamentary majority. However most legislation in the Japanese system is drafted by the relevant Ministry, and this is particularly so with respect to international trade matters dominated by MITI.[45] There would seem to be less tension between the executive and the parliament in this system, and it would appear more likely that the government could implement international agreements as well as other initiatives, since it would have considerable control over the parliamentary majority. Even in such a country, however, there are institutional power rivalries and tensions. The ruling party has a certain apparatus for its own decision-making, and this must be persuaded of the desirability of measures which require parliamentary approval. A Supreme Court in Japan presides over the legal conflicts, including constitutional rules. Although Japanese society has been described as less litigious than that of the US, and operates in a social climate that tends to discourage resort to formal court processes to resolve differences, other observers have noticed that a few cases relating to international economic measures have gone to the courts in Japan, and there has been speculation that this might increase.[46]

Some reflections
One interesting question is whether the different government struc-

ture of important GATT Contracting Parties affects the ability of those parties to negotiate effectively and efficiently in the GATT or in other international economic relations. Are some nations able to gain a negotiating advantage in the GATT rounds, for example, because their constitutional structure permits more efficient negotiating procedures? Is the US at a disadvantage because of the constraints which Congress imposes on the executive? How do these various constitutional systems impact on the potential evolution of the GATT system?

In the early 1970s, European diplomats questioned the US government procedures for approving and implementing the results of a GATT negotiation (remembering the instances when Congress had failed to approve prior GATT negotiating results).[47] The US responded by developing some special procedures (the 'fast track') for congressional approval of the Tokyo Round results, which worked well in 1979. One irony of the situation at the end of the Tokyo Round was that the major constitutional issues which clouded implementation occurred in the European Community and not in the US. The EC had a significant internal debate about the power or competence of its institutions to accept and implement the Tokyo Round agreements, which resulted in some ambiguous compromises.

The end of the Uruguay Round could also very well involve difficulty on some of these issues. For example, it is not completely settled in the EC how agreements on services will be accepted or implemented.

4

TRADE NEGOTIATIONS: IMPLICATIONS OF THE URUGUAY ROUND

4.1 The tariff-negotiating round of GATT

Clearly the most significant success of the GATT since 1947 has been the reduction of tariff levels among the Contracting Parties. For the most part this has occurred as a result of seven intensive negotiating rounds, beginning in Geneva in 1947. As a result of these rounds, tariffs on industrial products imported into the industrial nations have been reduced to a point where in the view of some economists they are no longer significant, with a few exceptions. The exceptions include some 'peak levels' of particular products where tariffs remain high, and also include certain relationships between close neighbour trading partners (such as the United States and Canada), where even a few percentage points of a tariff can influence investment and other economic decisions.

Table 3 summarizes the seven trade negotiating rounds held so far. The first five of these negotiating rounds concentrated primarily on tariffs. The sixth, the Kennedy Round, planned to look seriously at non-tariff barriers, but that aim was only minimally achieved.

The Tokyo Round in the 1970s was the first major negotiating round to make non-tariff barriers the priority objective of the negotiation. Negotiating in a multilateral context on the reduction of non-tariff barriers is much more complex than is the case for

Table 3 GATT negotiating rounds

Round	Dates	Number of countries	Value of trade covered
Geneva	1947	23	$10 billion
Annecy	1949	33	Unavailable
Torquay	1950	34	Unavailable
Geneva	1956	22	$2.5 billion
Dillon	1961-1	45	$4.9 billion
Kennedy	1962-7	48	$40 billion
Tokyo	1973-9	99	$155 billion

tariffs. As GATT became established, and tariffs were substantially reduced, non-tariff barriers became significantly more important. Many domestic producer interests began turning to a variety (more than a thousand) of non-tariff barriers as a way to minimize the competition from imports, since tariffs would no longer provide that type of protection.

The focus on non-tariff barriers, therefore, became a substantial challenge to the GATT 'constitution'. Not only was negotiation for reducing these barriers much more complex, thus requiring a different sort of institutional framework, but the implementation of any non-tariff measure agreements resulting from the negotiation was much more difficult to achieve. In the Tokyo Round, as mentioned in Chapter 3, nine different special agreements on non-tariff measures were completed, six or seven of which could have sometimes been called 'codes', since they involved reasonably concrete obligations. Nevertheless, the implementation of some of these codes has been very troubled for several reasons. First, some of the codes (particularly the agreement concerning subsidies) contain very ambiguous language, which reflects the lack of real agreement among the negotiating partners in the Tokyo Round. Secondly, the dispute settlement procedures sometimes contained in these codes have not always worked satisfactorily, or have been the subject of controversy in connection with choices whether a dispute should be brought under a general GATT procedure, or under a particular code procedure. Finally, the codes have added substantially to the administrative and institutional burden of GATT, possibly tripling the amount of activity involved. This has put a strain on some of the smaller, less developed countries. In addition, the whole question of the legal relationship of the codes to the GATT itself has been raised by this result.

4.2 The Uruguay Round

Since the completion of the Tokyo Round in 1979, it was obvious to most trade policy members that a new round would be necessary. Partly this is because of the 'bicycle theory' of trade policy, namely that unless there is forward movement, the bicycle will fall over. If there were no initiatives on trade policy, the temptations of national governments to backslide would be very great. But in addition, the world was becoming increasingly complex and interdependent, and it was becoming more and more obvious that the GATT rules were not satisfactorily providing the measure of discipline that was needed to prevent tensions and damaging national activity. Very significant and substantial new subjects were proposed for GATT competence (including services and intellectual property) and these would require a prolonged period of consultation, diplomacy, and negotiation.

The declaration of Punta del Este contains the mandate for this new round,[1] and it is very broad indeed. The declaration was deemed a considerable success for the United States and a number of other countries who had been supporting a broad mandate. One of the key questions – whether services would be negotiated – was largely answered in the affirmative, though not without some compromise. Indeed, the inclusion of services in the negotiating round amply demonstrates the importance of institutional measures. The structure of the Punta del Este declaration makes it clear that the question of whether services would ultimately be part of the GATT structure (or that of some other organization) was left open by the declaration. Thus it is that the structure of the negotiation on the one hand deals with trade in goods, while setting up a separate committee and negotiating structure for trade in services. Nevertheless, as time goes on, it is the opinion of many officials and diplomats that the idea of the GATT system having competence over trade in services seems to be more widely accepted. Exactly what that means, however, is clearly not yet resolved. I have written elsewhere[2] that it would not be wise merely to amend the GATT so that it applies to services. Thus a separate agreement on services is very likely, along with a number of specific service sector agreements or chapters. At that point, it must be asked what sort of institutional mechanism will serve these services agreements and whether the GATT Secretariat will also serve them.

After Punta del Este, the Contracting Parties established 14 negotiating groups to work on the problems of trade in goods,[3] and a separate structure was set up for negotiations on trade in services. An elaborate meeting schedule was formulated, and governments geared up to handle these meetings.

It was soon decided there would be a mid-term review towards the end of 1988, which would be a meeting of GATT Contracting Party Ministers of Trade, to survey progress and establish directions for the remainder of the negotiation. Originally it was thought that there might be some concrete agreements that could be accepted and possibly even implemented as a result of the mid-term review, but in the end there were no real agreements to be implemented, with the possible exception of some improvements in the dispute settlement process. Rather the agreements set forth the framework of the further negotiations.

The mid-term review was held in December 1988 in Montreal on the basis of draft texts prepared by each of the negotiating committees. Some of these were very elaborate; others were rather short and cursory. Some of the texts were heavily laden with 'square brackets' of alternative provisions. At the end of the Montreal meeting it was announced that agreement had not been reached. Certain texts had been accepted, but some countries were not prepared to accept those unless all other texts were also accepted, and there was considerable controversy with respect to certain key issues, including agriculture. Consequently, it was decided that the GATT Director-General would try to get the various Contracting Parties to establish agreement on a final text, and this occurred after some meetings in Geneva in April 1989.

It is not surprising that there was a lack of agreement at Montreal. The two largest trading blocs were represented at that meeting by officials who were leaving their positions. In the United States, the November 1988 presidential election had established that the Bush Administration would succeed the Reagan Administration, but Reagan officials were still in charge at Montreal, and it was not always clear who their successors would be. Likewise and coincidentally, in the European Economic Community Frans Andriessen was about to replace Willy De Clercq as Commissioner for External Relations (the counterpart of the US trade negotiator). As it turned out, there was a bit of reciprocal and symmetrical irony with respect to these two trading powers: in the US the trade representative, Clayton Yeutter, became Secretary of Agriculture. In the EC, the Commissioner for Agriculture, Frans Andriessen, became trade negotiator!

If the mid-term review was timed to occur shortly after the US presidential elections as a way for the GATT Contracting Parties to reconnoitre the situation in the light of the US election result, it may have afforded that opportunity to the Contracting Parties. The other side-effect, however, was to create an element of paralysis, or inability to make the necessary compromises in order to achieve an agreement at Montreal. Nevertheless, once the new administrations were in place, and since their positions were relatively uncompromised by their predecessors, they were able to move forward and achieve some sort of consensus. The result of this process, by the end of April 1989, was the set of agreements of the mid-term review.[4]

4.3 Implications of the Uruguay Round for the GATT 'constitution'

The Uruguay Round obviously presents fundamental institutional questions for the GATT. The Punta del Este declaration itself contains reference to these matters. The negotiating groups set up to address dispute settlement procedures and the 'functioning of the GATT system (FOGS)' are among these.

However, a number of other institutional issues are also raised by the declaration and the proposed course of the Uruguay Round negotiation. For example, as mentioned, the Punta del Este declaration called for several 'new issues' for negotiation, particularly on trade in services, intellectual property questions, and 'trade related investment measures'. All three of these, but particularly the first two, pose some important and fundamental institutional questions such as: Will the GATT system embrace trade in services? To what degree will the GATT system embrace intellectual property issues, and how will these relate to WIPO – the World Intellectual Property Organization?

In addition, at Punta del Este it was agreed that China would begin negotiating for entry (or re-entry) into the GATT system, and clearly the admittance of such a large state-trading country poses fundamental institutional and conceptual problems for the GATT.

Many of these developments will require the GATT Contracting

Parties, at the end of the Uruguay Round (now targeted for the end of 1990), to consider a whole series of GATT institutional questions, discussed later in this monograph. However, these characteristics of the Uruguay Round also suggest some opportunities for the GATT. As we will note in later chapters, an overall package result of the Uruguay Round could very well contain some fundamental GATT institutional reforms, and this might provide a much better chance for acceptance of such reforms than a piecemeal approach.

PART II

Perspectives on

International Economic Institutions

5

THE JURISPRUDENCE AND POLICY OF A GATT 'CONSTITUTION'

5.1 The institutional problems of GATT

We can now review a number of the institutional problems that are found in the GATT system, some of which we have discussed in previous chapters.

(1) We have seen that the fundamental treaty structure of the GATT is flawed on several counts. GATT application is still, after 40 years, 'provisional'. The GATT rules do apply as binding international treaty obligations, yet we still see statements to the contrary in a number of different places. The GATT also was and continues to be a subject of some dispute between the Congress and the executive branch in the United States. Furthermore, grandfather rights still exist, even though they were originally intended to be temporary. A number of other institutional problems stem from this basic flaw in treaty structure, including the problem of amendments, the relationship to domestic law, the dispute settlement procedure, questions of membership, and problems of rule-making and power of the Contracting Parties.

(2) The amending provisions of the basic treaty structure are such that it is now rarely considered possible to amend the GATT. The delay required by the treaty acceptance process, the difficulty of obtaining the required number of acceptances, the shift in bargaining power involved under the amending procedure in the context of a large membership, and the fact that even when an amendment is

effective in GATT it will not apply to countries which do not accept, are all reasons why the amending procedure has fallen into disuse. This has caused a certain rigidity and inability to develop rules so as to accommodate the many new developments in international trade and other economic interdependence subjects. One result has been the development of an elaborate system of 'side treaties', which create some of their own problems. What will be the approach in the Uruguay Round remains to be seen.

(3)   A key problem is the relationship to GATT of these many side agreements, in most cases stand-alone treaties which are intimately linked to the GATT treaty structure itself. It is unclear in some circumstances what this relationship is, and whether an obligation contained in the side agreement will prevail over that of the GATT or vice versa. In any event, since the side agreements tend to have a series of separate procedures for various matters including dispute settlement, there is a certain inefficiency in the potential 'forum shopping'.

(4)   The relationship of the GATT treaty system to domestic law in a number of GATT member countries is very murky. Some problems may be unavoidable, since the national legal systems differ so widely. Nevertheless, some attention could be given to the possibility of introducing certain international treaty obligations with respect to how the trade and economic rules should be implemented domestically. Increasing attention has been given to this question in recent years, sometimes under the rubric 'transparency'. It should be noted that the GATT agreement itself has several clauses (Articles VIII and IX) that are related to this question.

(5)   There are a number of problems concerning membership or contracting party status in the GATT system, including its large number of side agreements. There are various ways by which a nation becomes a member of GATT or one of the side agreements. In some cases, membership can be obtained by a territory that does not have full independent international sovereignty. Former colonies can be sponsored for membership and enter the GATT with very little substantive commitment, reducing the terrain of reciprocity and leading to criticisms of unfairness. The GATT has an opt-out clause (Article XXXV) by which individual GATT Contracting Parties can opt out of a GATT relationship with other parties, at one time only (when one of them originally enters

GATT). Nevertheless, there are a number of instances where there is an effective opt-out at a later time, with murky legal results. Article XXI, with an exception for 'national security' purposes, is related to this issue.

(6) The power of the CONTRACTING PARTIES defined in the GATT agreement is very ambiguous. Indeed, it is so broad that it could be the subject of abuse (but it has not so far been abused). There are a number of unsettled and disquieting issues, such as the power of the Contracting Parties to interpret the GATT agreement; and the relationship of actions of the Contracting Parties to some of the side agreements. Furthermore, the decision-making process leaves much to be desired. The so-called 'consensus approach' has some inherent defects, but has evolved to ameliorate some of the problems of a one-nation one-vote structure, coupled with the ambiguity and terseness of the GATT text. The GATT Council has been created by resolution of the CONTRACTING PARTIES, and has no treaty status.

(7) The dispute settlement processes of GATT have been among the more intriguing institutional evolutions of that institution. The treaty language is very sparse indeed, but many decades of practice have resulted in a considerable amount of exegesis, and the elaboration of much of this in a Tokyo Round 'understanding', as well as further efforts to improve the procedures during the current Uruguay Round. Dispute settlement procedures are intimately connected with problems of 'effectiveness'. There is considerable concern about whether the GATT procedures can stand up to some of the pressures that are currently being imposed upon them.

(8) Finally, there has long been a problem with respect to the relationship of GATT to the other Bretton Woods institutions, particularly the International Monetary Fund and the World Bank. This is one of the items explicitly flagged for negotiation in the Uruguay Round, and certainly merits more attention, since the monetary questions are really only the other side of the coin of trade questions.

5.2 The fundamental nature of a charter

International institutions consistently pose some difficult and perplexing questions about the structuring of human affairs. National governments traditionally cling to sovereignty, and often hesitate to relinquish any ground to international institutions. This reluctance is often related to the size and power of the nation concerned, as well as to the relative influence of key interest groups within such nations. Traditionally, smaller nations and weaker interest groups have been somewhat more willing to look beyond their national borders for institutional measures that would assist them to redress their relative lack of power. There are sometimes exceptions. For example, the United States, after a period in the early part of this century in which it turned away from international ties, has since World War II been a leader in the development of international institutions. There are at least two reasons for this. First, a wealthy nation has a great deal at stake in the peace and relative absence of armed conflict in a troubled and turbulent world. Secondly, the US constitution already provides for a considerable amount of internal conflict and tension, and sometimes one part of the US government (particularly the Congress) may feel that its interests are actually better protected by hemming in another part of the government (such as the executive branch) by international obligations. Likewise, the reverse can be a motivation.

In any event, the concept of sovereignty is changing dramatically, and begins to lose most of its meaning, at least in the context of economic affairs, now that the world is so interdependent economically.

Different approaches to international affairs can be seen reflected in different kinds of models of international institutions. Broadly, one can see two types of models. First is a model of an international institution that is primarily a forum for discussion and future negotiation. Such an institution tends to have neither many concrete or precisely defined international rules or obligations, nor a mechanism for implementing or enforcing such obligations. To some extent, one can view the OECD as representing this model.

A contrary model is an international institution that provides concrete and reasonably precise rules which governments feel are necessary. In the area of economic activity many such institutions exist. Most prominent, of course, are the International Monetary Fund and a number of specialized agencies such as ICAO (regarding transport activity), and the Universal Postal Union. When the ITO Charter was drafted at Geneva and Havana in 1947–8, it was clearly intended that the international institution would contain fairly precise rules, and that there would be a mechanism for implementing or enforcing them. The GATT has been gradually gravitating towards this latter model.

When we contemplate the constitutional problems and difficulties of the GATT system today, and thus explore various options for improving that system, this discussion of the appropriate international institution becomes central. Indeed, as will be discussed below, governments and even individuals are not always clear which model they prefer. The US government, for example, has during the last 15 years been articulating the need for improving the GATT dispute settlement process and rule implementation. Yet in practice the United States has been quite willing to attempt to subvert that process, by a variety of procedural devices or simply by refusing to comply with the results of the panel procedure which went against it. In some of these cases, however, the United States ultimately 'comes around', to its credit. As this is written, there are at least four outstanding GATT 'judgments' that United States action is inconsistent with GATT, and several more procedures have been started that may end in similar judgments.[1] It is thus fair to ask how serious the United States is about its desire to see and enhance dispute settlement procedure in the GATT.

Other governments do not escape this type of criticism either. The European Economic Community has been one of the most ardent opponents of improvement in the GATT dispute settlement process during the last 15 years. A variety of reasons for that can be given, and it may be that these attitudes within the EC power structure are beginning to shift towards more tolerance of an enhanced GATT dispute procedure. Some have noted that a number of EC successes in panel proceedings may be influencing these EC attitudes. The EC seems now more disposed to bring its own complaints into the GATT procedures than was true in earlier years.

It is thus quite possible to be undecided about the fundamental nature which an international institution regarding economic matters should have, and consequently worth examining more closely some of the policy objectives that relate to this fundamental question.

5.3 Rule- or power-oriented diplomacy

Although international law rules may be somewhat less effective than their domestic counterparts, at least for those nations with stable legal systems and a generally effective central government, it is not always the case that domestic laws are implemented efficiently. It is important for the policy adviser, the statesman, or practitioner, accurately to evaluate the real impact of the international rules, recognizing that some of those rules (often the ones that do not reach the headlines) do have considerable effect and influence on real government and business decisions.[2] For example, despite cynical statements by members of the US Congress that GATT rules are 'irrelevant', there are a number of proven instances when congressional committees and their staff members have taken considerable trouble to tailor legislative proposals so as to minimize the risk of a complaint to GATT. Not all of these efforts have been successful, but in other cases Congress has been persuaded to drop a proposal because of its inconsistency with GATT provisions.[3] The US executive branch is also influenced by GATT legality arguments, although it too does not always defer to these.

The ability of nations unilaterally to apply measures such as antidumping or countervailing duties often has a powerful influence on potential transactions or even on government policy. The constraints on the nation applying such duties stem from the GATT and MTN code rules on those subjects, and thus these rules are relevant in determining what would be the likely response of an importing country to certain dumping or subsidy-like practices in an exporting country.

In addition to the question of evaluating the effectiveness of existing international rules, there are several important policy issues about rule implementation, which are seldom explicitly addressed. First, should the legal system be improved to make rules more effective? Secondly, should new rules be added and made more effective? These questions are not necessarily trivial, or to be answered in the affirmative. To put this another way, realistic observations of the operation of the legal system, even as it pertains to international economic affairs, will lead one to perceive that many government and private practitioners are not always in favour of an effective international rules system.[4]

Why is there real (albeit sometimes concealed or implicit) opposition to the effectiveness of international rules? Some of the reason for this can be traced to the older concepts of national sovereignty. Furthermore, the international rules do cause real difficulties for national leaders. It is harder to deliver on promises to constituents. Several situations lead even the wise national leader to cause his government to breach or consider breaching the international rules.

One of these is the case when the international 'rule' is patently unfair or bad policy. This may be because the rule is out-dated and not in tune with current actual practice and conditions. It may also be because the current international rule-making process is faulty – as happens when voting procedures allow unrealistic rules to be that do not adequately recognize real power relationships.[5]

Another situation in which it can be argued that rules *should* be breached is when reform of the rule is badly needed, but the international and national institutional system for some reason makes the reform impossible. It could be argued that the US departure from the currency par value system of the IMF in 1971 was such a case, leading quickly to a major revision in the IMF Charter to allow 'floating exchange rates', which had been advocated for decades by many eminent economists.[6]

Nevertheless, every departure from the rules carries some risks. It causes respect for the rule system itself to be weakened, and facilitates departure from the rules in the next difficulty. If rules are viewed as one tool for ordering or improving human affairs, then weakening a rule system tends to reduce the utility of that tool in all its contexts.

One way to explore the questions raised above is to compare two techniques of modern diplomacy: a 'rule-oriented' technique, and a 'power-oriented' technique. This perhaps puts the issue too simply (because in practice the observable international institutions and legal systems involve some mixture of both), but it is nevertheless an useful way to examine the policy issues involved. The matter can be explained as follows:

> In broad perspective one can roughly divide the various techniques for the peaceful settlement of international disputes into two types: settlement by negotiation and agreement with reference (explicitly or implicitly) to relative power status of the parties; or settlement by negotiation or decision with reference to norms or rules to which both parties have previously agreed.
>
> For example, countries A and B have a trade dispute regarding B's treatment of imports from A to B of widgets. The first technique mentioned would involve a negotiation between A and B by which the most powerful of the two would have the advantage. Foreign aid, military maneuvers, or import restrictions on other key goods by way of retaliation would figure in

the negotiation. A small country would hesitate to challenge a large one on whom its trade depends. Implicit or explicit threats (e.g. to impose quantitative restrictions on some other product) would be a major part of the technique employed. Domestic political influences would probably play a greater weight in the approach of the respective negotiators in this system, particularly on the negotiator for the more powerful party.

On the other hand, the second technique suggested – reference to agreed rules – would see the negotiators arguing about the application of the rule (e.g. was B obligated under a treaty to allow free entry of A's goods in question?). During the process of negotiating a settlement it would be necessary for the parties to understand that an unsettled dispute would ultimately be resolved by impartial third party judgments based on the rules so that the negotiators would be negotiating with reference to their respective predictions as to the outcome of those judgments and not with reference to potential retaliation or actions exercising power of one or more of the parties to the dispute.

In both techniques negotiation and private settlement of disputes is the dominant mechanism for resolving differences; but the key is the perception of the participants as to what are the 'bargaining chips'. Insofar as agreed rules for governing the economic relations between the parties exist, a system which predicates negotiation on the implementation of those rules would seem for a number of reasons to be preferred. The mere existence of the rules, however, is not enough. When the issue is the application or interpretation of those rules (as compared with the formulation of new rules), it is necessary for the parties to believe that if their negotiations reach an impasse the settlement mechanisms which take over for the parties will be designed to fairly apply or interpret the rules. If no such system exists, then the parties are left basically to rely upon their respective 'power positions', tempered (it is hoped) by the good will and good faith of the more powerful party (cognizant of his long range interests). . . .

All diplomacy, and indeed all government, involves a mixture of these techniques. To a large degree, the history of civilization may be described as a gradual evolution from a power oriented approach, in the state of nature, towards a rule oriented approach. However, never is the extreme in either case reached.

In modern Western democracies, as we know them, power continues to play a major role, particularly political power of voter acceptance, but also to a lesser degree economic power such as labor unions or large corporations. However, these governments have passed far along the scale towards a rule oriented approach, and generally have an elaborate legal system involving court procedures and a monopoly of force through a police and a military, to insure the rules will be followed. The US government has indeed proceeded far in this direction, as the resignation of a recent President demonstrates. When one looks at the history of England over the last thousand years, I think that the evolutionary hypothesis from power to rule can be supported. And more recently when one looks at the evolution of the EC, one is struck by the evolution towards a system that is remarkably elaborate in its rule structure, effectuated through a Court of Justice, albeit without a monopoly of force.

In international affairs, a strong argument can be made that to a certain extent this same evolution must occur, even though currently it has not progressed very far. The initiatives of the World War II and immediate post-war period towards developing international institutions are part of this evolution, but as is true in most evolutions there have been set-backs, and mistakes have been made. Likewise, when one focuses on international economic policy, we find also that the dichotomy between power oriented diplomacy and rule oriented diplomacy can be seen. We have tried to develop rules, in the context of the International Monetary Fund and the GATT. The success has been varied.

Nevertheless, a particularly strong argument exists for pursuing gradually and consistently the progress of international economic affairs towards a rule-oriented approach. Apart from the advantages which accrue generally to international affairs through a rule oriented approach – less reliance on raw power and the temptation to exercise it or flex one's muscles which can get out of hand; a fairer break for the smaller countries, or at least a perception of greater fairness; the development of agreed procedures to achieve the necessary compromises; in economic affairs there are additional reasons.

Economic affairs tend (at least in peace time) to affect more citizens directly than may be the case for political and military affairs. Particularly as the world becomes more economically interdependent, more and more private citizens find their jobs, their businesses, and their quality of life affected if not controlled by forces from outside their country's boundaries. Thus they are more affected by the economic policy pursued by their own country on their behalf. In addition, the relationships become increasingly complex – to the point of being incomprehensible to even the brilliant human mind. As a result, citizens assert themselves, at least within a democracy, and require their representatives and government officials to respond to their needs and their perceived complaints. The result of this is increasing citizen participation, and more parliamentary or congressional participation in the processes of international economic policy, thus restricting the degree of power and discretion which the Executive possesses.

This makes international negotiations and bargaining increasingly difficult. However, if citizens are going to make their demands be heard and have their influence, a 'power-oriented' negotiating process (often requiring secrecy, and executive discretion so as to be able to formulate and implement the necessary compromises) becomes more difficult if not impossible. Consequently, the only appropriate way to turn seems to be toward a rule-oriented system, whereby the various layers of citizens, parliaments, executives and international organizations will all have their inputs, arriving tortuously to a rule, which however, when established will enable business and other decentralized decision makers to rely upon the stability and predictability of governmental activity in relation to the rule.[7]

5.4 Why worry about the 'constitution'?

It can be (and is) asked, 'why worry about the legal rules of international economic relations?' Sometimes a speaker goes on to say, 'the rules don't matter; as long as the participants have the political will to make the system succeed, it will do so'.

At best, this perspective is shallow. A major purpose of human institutions is to prevent the disaster that occurs precisely when the 'political will' to act constructively is absent. Institutions must be designed to withstand the 'worst-case scenarios'; not just to operate with the best-case ones. People and power groups will always be tempted to undermine the system if by doing so major short-term advantages will be obtained.

Furthermore, the writings about negotiation and bargaining strategies, some of them explicating such strategies in the context of the 'prisoner's dilemma' paradigm,[8] demonstrate that in certain situations analogous to the conditions of international trade, participants will be tempted to take actions that will seem to maximize their own return only to learn that opposing participants will do so also, with the result that both lose. The way out is to agree on a set of restraining rules.

But beyond these principles, there is a set of more general arguments which strongly support a 'rule-oriented constitution' for the conduct of international economic affairs. The former GATT chief economist Jan Tumlir ably expresses this:

> International trade as a large-scale activity requires careful planning and substantial investments, which can be recouped only over long periods of time. All long-term investments are highly sensitive to uncertainty, and foreign-trade-related investments doubly so for their outcomes may be affected by policy changes in several countries. The trade part of the international economy order can thus be understood as a set of policy commitments exchanges between and among countries in order to minimize policy-generated uncertainty and so to maximize the gains from trade.
>
> .   .   .   .
>
> Historically, this set of commitments evolved as a series of contractual bargains.
>
> .   .   .   .
>
> Without the judge and bailiff in the background, contracts do not mean much.[9]

6

RULE APPLICATION AND DISPUTE SETTLEMENT

6.1 Interpretations and rule application

In addition to a procedure for formulating rules, a 'legal system', including one based on treaties, needs a procedure for applying the rules. This involves the interpretation or 'individualization' of rules by which individual cases are decided, and this in turn involves a 'dispute settlement' process.

The principles of treaty interpretation include 'ordinary meaning' of the words, other agreements or instruments influencing the treaty which were accepted by the parties to the treaty at the time it was concluded, subsequent agreement between the parties to the treaty, 'subsequent practice in the application of the treaty which establishes the agreement of the parties regarding its interpretation', and other relevant rules of international law. In some circumstances the preparatory work can also be relevant.[1]

Each of these principles of interpretation plays a role in the GATT and associated agreements. The original GATT contains an Annexe with a series of agreed interpretations which are considered definitive.[2] Subsequently there have been formal agreements which purport to interpret the GATT. Among these are the Tokyo Round Subsidies and Anti-Dumping Codes, although these clearly go beyond mere interpretation. Whether these codes can influence the GATT interpretation for Contracting Parties which do not accept the codes is not yet clear.[3]

Technically, to be 'binding', practice must be sufficient to 'establish the agreement of the parties'. Exactly how far the evidence must go in this regard is not clear. Additionally it should be noted that under accepted doctrines of international law, *stare decisis* or the common-law concept of 'precedent' does not apply.[4] Thus a World Court decision in a dispute between countries A and B provides no binding precedent as such in a dispute between C and D, nor between A and C, nor even for another dispute at another time between A and B.[5] Yet in practice, the diplomats and officials who participate in the GATT system are very much influenced by precedent, and often mention precedents in some detail in GATT deliberations, as well as in the formal dispute settlement panel 'findings'. A common-law lawyer would find himself very much at home in many GATT legal discussions!

From time to time GATT interpretations have been made in a short statement by the Chairman of the Contracting Parties.[6] Sometimes these are made in the context of a 'consensus view' of the CPs, without objection from any CP, sometimes as a statement of the Chair without any explicit connection to an agreement or a 'vote' (without objection) of the CPs. In all such cases, however, it is safe to assume that the text has been carefully negotiated in advance and deemed acceptable to the interested CPs. Similarly, dispute settlement panel 'findings' will often contain rulings interpreting the GATT application in the particular dispute, and the CPs 'adopt' most of these findings. These may be binding on the disputing parties, but it can still be asked what is the status of such 'interpretative statements' as to future disputes. Although their status is quite indefinite, the procedure suggests, in Vienna Convention phraseology, 'practice ... establishing agreement'.[7] (More on this later.)

Another important question is whether the CONTRACTING PARTIES of GATT, under their Article XXV powers, have the authority to make a legal and binding interpretation of GATT. Some international organizations are explicitly given such power in their charters, such that an interpretation adopted by the procedure specified would carry with it a binding treaty obligation to accept the interpretation even for nations disagreeing with the interpretation and even in the absence of sufficient practice to establish 'agreement of the parties'.[8]

The language of GATT itself does not explicitly grant this power, although it gives authority to the Contracting Parties for 'joint action' with a view to 'facilitating the operation and furthering the objectives of this Agreement'. This language seems broad enough to include the power to interpret, but caution is necessary for several reasons. First, since binding interpretative power for other organizations has been explicit in their charters, the absence of explicit power in the GATT could argue against the existence of that power. Second, the ill-fated ITO charter contained explicit provisions for interpretations, whereas these provisions were not included in the GATT (because the GATT was not considered to be an 'organization').[9] In the light of the Vienna Convention's codification of customary international law, as well as the general language of GATT Article XXV, it would seem likely that at least where there is no formal dissent by any GATT CP, various 'practice' actions of the GATT would be deemed very definitive interpretations. In the case where the majority of CPs agree, but without unanimity, there is still some ambiguity. It is possible that the practice of GATT in its four decades of existence has itself established an interpretation of the Article XXV powers to include the power to interpret.

No dispute involving GATT or its associated agreements has ever been taken to the World Court (i.e., the International Court of Justice or ICJ).[10] It can be asked whether that court would have jurisdiction over such a dispute, or whether the internal GATT interpretative processes would be held to be exclusive. The ITO charter would have provided both a requirement to use exclusively its own dispute procedures and also a reference to the ICJ in certain circumstances.[11] No such provisions are included in the GATT, but in any event no GATT Contracting Party has yet been motivated to bring a GATT case to the ICJ.[12]

Questions similar to these can be asked regarding the agreements resulting from the Tokyo Round negotiations, and the answers are even more difficult. The agreements themselves do not explicitly grant the power of formal binding interpretation, although many of them have dispute settlement procedures. The agreements do not contain the phrase found in GATT Article XXV, so no claim on that basis can be made.[13] The phraseology of the procedures contained in the GATT side agreements varies greatly, sometimes calling for exclusive procedures[14] and at other times 'permitting' use of specified procedures.[15]

6.2 GATT dispute settlement procedures

(a) The fundamental goal of GATT dispute settlement procedures: negotiation or rule application?

One of the more controversial aspects of the GATT as an institution is its dispute settlement mechanism. It is probably fair to say that this mechanism is unique. It is also flawed, owing in part to the troubled beginnings of GATT. Yet these procedures have worked better than might be expected[16], and it is possible to argue that they have also worked better than those of the World Court. A number of interesting policy questions are raised by the experience of the procedure, not the least of which is the question as to what should be the fundamental objective of the system – to solve the instant dispute (by conciliation, obfuscation, power-threats, or otherwise), or to promote certain longer-term goals. In this section we will look at some of the fundamental policy controversies about the dispute settlement procedures of GATT, and then examine those procedures and those of GATT-associated agreements. In the next section we will explore how the system has worked.

The difference of opinion about the basic purpose or goal of the dispute settlement process in the GATT system has not often been explicit, and the same individuals sometimes express a preference for different approaches without realizing it. Of course, the matter is more one of appropriate balance along a spectrum than it is of choosing one extreme or the other, but nevertheless it is important to understand the difference. Perhaps the following two statements can help:

[A]s a part of the increasingly pragmatic policies of the secretariat and the recognition by all contracting parties that legalism does not contribute to trade liberalization, emphasis has shifted from the formal role of the GATT as third-party arbiter to its informal role as catalyst for the resolution of disputes by the disputing parties themselves.[17]

[I]nternational economic policy commitments, in the form of

agreed rules, have far-reaching domestic effects. . . . They are
the element which secures the ultimate co-ordination and
mutual compatibility of the purely domestic economic policies.
They form the basis from which the government can arbitrate
and secure an equitable and efficient balance between the
diverse domestic interests: producers v. consumers, export
industries v. import-competing industries. . . .[O]nly a firm
commitment to international rules makes possible the all-
important reconciliation, which I have already alluded to, of the
necessary balance on the production side and on the financial
side of the national economy.[18]

There are at least two important questions here: one historical,
one of future policy. The historical question is whether the goal of
dispute settlement established by GATT (through preparatory work
and practice) is oriented more towards 'conciliation and negotiation'
or towards 'rule integrity'. The future policy question is: which of
these *ought* to be the goal? These questions relate to the 'power- or
rule-oriented diplomacy' discussion in Chapter 5.

As to the first question, the record is somewhat mixed. Despite the
many statements of writers[19] and diplomats that the GATT is merely
a 'negotiating forum', primarily designed to 'preserve a balance of
concessions and obligations', there is considerable historical
evidence to the contrary. At least one draughtsman of GATT said at
the preparatory meetings that the agreement

should deal with these subjects in precise detail so that the
obligations of member governments would be clear and unam-
biguous. Most of these subjects readily lend themselves to such
treatment. Provisions on such subjects, once agreed upon,
would be self-executing and could be applied by the governments concerned without further elaboration or international
action.[20]

The original intention was for GATT to be placed in the institutional setting of the ITO, and the draft ITO charter called for a
rigorous dispute settlement procedure which contemplated effective
use of arbitration (not always mandatory, however), and even
appeal to the World Court in some circumstances.[21] Clair Wilcox,
Vice-Chairman of the US Delegation to the Havana Conference,

notes that the possibility of suspending trade concessions under this procedure was

> regarded as a method of restoring a balance of benefits and obligations that, for any reason, may have been disturbed. It is nowhere described as a penalty to be imposed on members who may violate their obligations or as a sanction to insure that these obligations will be observed. But even though it is not so regarded, it will operate in fact as a sanction and a penalty.[22]

He further notes the procedure for obtaining a World Court opinion on the law involved in a dispute, and says:

> A basis is thus provided for the development of a body of international law to govern trade relationships.[23]

The shift in GATT from a committee or 'working-party' procedure to a 'panel' procedure (see below), with its connotation of impartial third-party findings, can also be used as evidence that the practice evolved in a direction of 'rule integrity', and a number of panel reports in the first several decades of GATT contained reasoning which closely resembled that of an opinion of a court of law, with reference to precedent, etc. Then in the 1960s, the GATT dispute settlement procedure fell into disuse. Some CPs feared that invocation of the procedure would be deemed an 'unfriendly act', or for other prudent policy reasons abstained from formal procedures to resolve disputes. Countries with less bargaining power, however, seemed to feel differently. Indeed the developing countries pushed through a proposal in GATT designed to strengthen the dispute settlement procedures as they applied in disputes with developing countries.[24] In a celebrated exercise Uruguay brought a series of complaints on the treatment of its exports by industrial countries (with mixed results).[25] It was during this case that there developed the doctrine of 'prima facie nullification or impairment' (described below), which has had a continuing effect in GATT.

(b) The procedures of dispute settlement in GATT
The GATT, not intended to be an 'organization', has only a few paragraphs devoted to dispute settlement.[26] Although one can argue that there are a number of 'dispute settlement' procedures dis-

tributed throughout the GATT (raising the issue of what we mean by that phrase),[27] the central and formal procedures are found in Articles XXII and XXIII. The first of these simply establishes the right to consult with any other contracting party on matters related to the GATT, not apparently a major commitment but nevertheless a useful one. Indeed, Article XXII should be interpreted as ruling out the argument against allowing a request to consult on some potential legislative or executive action, because the matter was 'premature'.

Article XXIII is the centrepiece for dispute settlement. It also provides for consultation as a prerequisite to invoke the multilateral GATT processes. Three features of these processes should be stressed: (1) they may usually be invoked on grounds of 'nullification or impairment' of benefits expected under the Agreement, and do *not* depend on actual breach of legal obligation; (2) they establish the power for the CONTRACTING PARTIES not only to investigate and recommend action, but to 'give a ruling on the matter'; and (3) they give the CONTRACTING PARTIES the power in appropriately serious cases to authorize 'a contracting party or parties' to suspend GATT obligations to other Contracting Parties. Each of these features has important interpretations and implications, and although Article XXIII does not say much more than this, the procedures followed to implement these principles have evolved over the four decades of practice into a rather elaborate process, which, as noted earlier, has been fairly, although not completely, successful.

The key to invoking the GATT dispute settlement mechanism is almost always 'nullification or impairment',[28] an unfortunately ambiguous phrase. It is neither sufficient nor necessary to find a 'breach of obligation' under this heading, although later practice has made this important. An early case in GATT[29] defined this 'nullification or impairment' (N or I) to include actions by a Contracting Party which harmed the trade of another, and 'could not reasonably have been anticipated' by the other at the time it negotiated for a concession. Thus the concept of 'reasonable expectations' was introduced, almost a 'contract'-type concept.[30] Even this elaboration becomes very ambiguous. Consequently a later practice in GATT developed the enumeration of three situations in which the CPs and their panels would find 'prima facie nullification or impairment'. One of these situations was the breach of an obligation. The other two were the use of domestic subsidies to eliminate imports in certain cases[31] and the use of quantitative restrictions (even when otherwise legal in GATT).[32] In such cases, the burden of proof of showing that no N or I occurred as the result of the breach, subsidy, or quantitative restriction, shifted to the country which breached or used those actions. Without a clear showing that no N or I occurred, the GATT practice assumes that the panel is bound to make a prima facie N or I ruling, usually calling for the offending nation to bring its actions into conformity with the GATT obligation. For example, when the US imposed a tax on imports of certain oil products which was higher than the tax it imposed on like products produced domestically, even though the revenue earned seemed very small, a GATT panel ruled[33] that the technical inconsistency of the tax with GATT obligations meant that the US must assume the burden of showing there was no nullification or impairment, rather than that the complaining party be obliged to show that N or I existed. In that case, the US was unable to sustain its burden, and the panel ruled against the US. (Congress is currently considering legislation to bring this tax into conformity with the GATT as interpreted by the panel.)

When GATT was first established, disputes would generally be taken up by the biannual plenary meeting of the Contracting Parties. Later they would be brought to an 'Intersessional Committee' of the CPs, and even later delegated to a working party set up to examine either all disputes, or only a particular dispute brought to GATT.[34] Around 1955 a major shift in the procedure occurred, largely because of the influence of the then Director-General, Eric Wyndham-White.[35] It was decided that rather than using a working party which was composed of nations (so that each could designate the person who would represent it, subject to that government's instructions), a dispute would be referred to a panel of experts. The three or five experts would be specifically named and should act in their own capacity and not as representatives of any government. This development represented a shift from what was primarily a 'negotiating' atmosphere of multilateral diplomacy, to a more 'arbitration'-oriented procedure designed impartially to arrive at the truth and the best interpretation of the law. Almost all subsequent dispute procedures in GATT have used a panel in this fashion.[36]

Although the CONTRACTING PARTIES are authorized (by majority vote) to suspend concessions (by way of retorsion, retaliation, or 're-balancing' of benefits), they have hitherto done so in only one case.

This was the result of a 1951 complaint brought by the Netherlands against the United States for the latter's use of import restraints on dairy products imported from the Netherlands, contrary to GATT.[37] For seven consecutive years, the Netherlands was authorized to use restraints against importation of US grain as 'sanction or compensation', although it never acted on that authorization. This had no effect on US action, however. Recently there have been some moves to seek authorization to suspend obligations,[38] and the US has also taken measures without authorization.[39]

During the Tokyo Round negotiation, some initiative was taken to improve the dispute settlement processes of the GATT. The so-called 'Framework Group Committee' of the negotiation was given this task, among others. However, partly because of the strong objection of the EC to any changes in the existing procedures, this effort did not get very far. The result was a document entitled 'Understanding regarding Notification, Consultation, Dispute Settlement and Surveillance', which was adopted by the CONTRACT-ING PARTIES at their 35th Session in Geneva in November 1979.[40] Like the other understandings resulting from the Tokyo Round, the precise legal status of this is not clear. Unlike the Tokyo Round 'codes' and other agreements, it is not a stand-alone treaty and neither is it a 'waiver' under Article XXV of GATT. It is presumably adopted under the general powers of that Article to 'facilitate the operation and further the objectives' of GATT. This document and its Annexe nevertheless form a sort of code of procedure for the dispute settlement practices of GATT.

The salient features of this 'restatement' of procedures are (1) the explicit provision for a conciliator role for the GATT Director-General; (2) the provision for panels (with some ambiguity about whether a complainant has a right to a panel); (3) reinforcement of the prima facie nullification or impairment concepts; (4) the outline of the work of a panel, including oral and written advocacy; (5) the permitted use of non-government persons on panels, though with a preference for government persons; (6) recognition of the practice of issuing a panel report with statement of facts and rationale; and (7) understanding that the report is then submitted to the CONTRACTING PARTIES for final approval.

Subsequent to the 1979 understanding, there has continued to be much dissatisfaction in GATT about the dispute settlement procedures.

Complaints have included the following:

(1) procedures tend to drag on (sometimes for years);
(2) it is difficult to find appropriate panellists;
(3) a losing party may block adoption of a panel report by the Council because of the 'consensus' rule;
(4) some panels have written imprecise reports or 'split differences' instead of making sound, reasoned findings;
(5) there have been one or two unfortunate instances of improper pressure put upon certain panellists by a government;
(6) some governments have taken a long time to implement the changes in their law necessary to make that law consistent with GATT as interpreted by the panel;
(7) there have been disputes about which procedure (GATT or a 'code') must be pursued.

Some of these problems have been greatly ameliorated by certain reforms already undertaken, such as the use of non-government panellists to increase the availability of panellists, and reformed secretariat procedures to speed up the process and to assist the panels in improving their legal reasoning.

Resolutions of the 1988 Montreal ministerial meeting contain some improvements.[41] For example, the Montreal terminology made it somewhat clearer that a complaining party had a right to a panel proceeding. It also established a new optional arbitration procedure, under which disputing parties could agree to abide by the arbitration award. It confirmed that the GATT Director-General has authority to step in and form a panel when the consultations of the parties break down on this point. Furthermore, it firmed up the timetable for a panel procedure in an effort to have it completed within nine months. However, as to the all-important question of council adoption of a panel report, the procedural weakness which allowed a losing party to block consensus appears to continue. Presumably further improvements in the procedure will be discussed during the remainder of the negotiation.

(c) GATT dispute settlement in practice

Dispute settlement activities in GATT have had their ups and downs. The process began as a relatively informal one, then began to use formal and objective third-party panels, and gradually developed not only procedural but substantive legal concepts.

In the 1960s the use of GATT dispute settlement procedures

declined, but in the following decade the United States began to bring a number of cases in GATT (partly reflecting its internal law which called for the use of this process),[42] and during and after the Tokyo Round many more cases have been brought, so that at times more than a dozen were simultaneously under way in GATT. As previously mentioned, both the 1982 ministerial meeting and subsequent proposals for the Uruguay Round of trade negotiations have emphasized the need to strengthen the procedures for dispute settlement, generally in the direction of 'rule integrity' rather than 'negotiation/conciliation'. Indeed, some diplomats have suggested privately that most developing countries as well as many industrial ones (including the US and most smaller independent countries) appeared to favour strengthening the dispute procedures, leaving the EC almost alone in open opposition, and, as noted before, the EC opposition may be softening. EC reluctance to embrace stronger dispute settlement procedure may have been related to views of some EC officials about the nature of GATT (preferring the idea of a 'negotiating' body), a traditional reluctance of bigger powers to yield 'sovereignty', and a preoccupation with internal constitutional developments compared to external economic relations. On the other hand, it must be recognized that actions by the US in recent years have undermined the rule integrity of GATT despite earlier statements of US officials supporting GATT rules.

From a study designed to itemize all disputes formally brought to GATT under Article XXIII or under another GATT agreement,[43] it appears that as of 1988 the number of cases initiated was approximately 233, of which 9 were brought under the MTN Code provisions (not the GATT itself). Of the cases for which further data exist, approximately 42 (18%) were settled or withdrawn before a panel or working party was constituted, and another group was settled or withdrawn before a panel or working party reported its findings. In all, panel or working party reports were completed in about 90 cases.

Of the panel reports forwarded to the CONTRACTING PARTIES, most were 'adopted'. Some others were merely 'noted', or otherwise not explicitly approved (although none was explicitly rejected), and several are still pending. The procedure of 'adoption' by the CPs is one of the most troublesome parts of the current procedure, since the losing Contracting Party can generally block acceptance by refusing to join in a 'consensus' decision to accept. Of the findings approved, all but a few have gained compliance, although in some cases compliance took many years to achieve. Nevertheless, some of the cases of non-compliance are very significant and troublesome.

Who brings the cases? Against whom? About what? The inventory study shows some revealing information. Over 76% of complaints are by industrial countries, and nearly 88% of the complaints are against industrial countries. Of the 50 complaints brought by industrial countries and LDCs, 47 or 94% are against industrial countries. Of the 179 complaints brought by industrial countries, 24 or 13% are against developing countries. The procedure is thus so far primarily used by or against industrial countries.

The importance of agriculture products in the dispute settlement cases is clear, especially with regard to cases brought against the EC. Likewise the article of GATT most frequently invoked is Article XI, which concerns the obligation not to use quotas. GATT Articles III (national treatment) and XVI (subsidies) also figure prominently in the disputes. Separate proceedings under MTN code procedures have not yet had much time to develop, but there have already been a number of cases under the Subsidies Code.

Although the compliance record of GATT panel recommendations is very respectable (perhaps higher in percentage terms than the World Court),[44] there has been much concern in recent years about non-compliance. It is very difficult to assemble data on this question, but my explorations suggest that of approximately 117 cases for which information is available, only about 8 to 10 have resulted in panel reports which have not been followed.[45] In some cases, the concerns about the GATT processes are partly to blame: a disputing nation can block 'adoption' of a report and then argue that there is no binding requirement for it to follow the report. Furthermore, merely counting cases does not adequately reveal their relative importance. If compliance occurs only in the relatively unimportant cases, the percentage record may look good but have little significance.

(d) The 'precedent effect' of GATT panel reports

We can now review a question about the legal effect of GATT panel reports that comes up from time to time. The panels tend to refer to earlier reports and indeed to use them in their reasoning almost as if they were binding precedents. But, as we have seen, under international law there is no such doctrine. Consequently, to appraise the effect of the GATT panel reports requires a somewhat more subtle analysis.

First, although most panel reports are 'adopted' by the Contracting Parties, some are not. Thus, we can start by asking what is the effect of those panel reports which are not adopted. It would seem that such reports would not be particularly influential in the GATT and would not even bind the parties to the particular dispute as to that dispute itself. (The contrary could be the case if the parties had agreed in advance to abide by the panel report, or perhaps to accept arbitration under the new Uruguay Round mid-term review procedures.) Furthermore, it seems clear that the unadopted report is in no way a 'decision' of the Contracting Parties, but it may have some influence because it is well reasoned and the panellists have a high reputation. Thus, even such a panel report could conceivably be part of the overall practice of GATT, which could be used at some future time in interpreting the GATT. This would be particularly so when, after time elapsed, it appeared that most or all Contracting Parties had accepted the implications of the panel report. Yet, if even one Contracting Party involved in the panel proceeding remained adamantly opposed to it, general principles of international law would suggest that that party would not be bound, and furthermore such holding out would undermine the practice.

Turning to the more interesting question of an adopted panel report, it would seem reasonably clear (although not certain) that the implications of the practice of GATT under its dispute settlement procedures suggest that the report is binding at least on the particular parties to the dispute as to that particular dispute. Still, of course, the report does not have *stare decisis* or precedent effect, even though future panels may refer to it approvingly, and follow its reasoning. Thus the report may have 'persuasive effect'.

Does it have any stronger effect? Clearly it is now part of the practice of GATT. Thus, it becomes part of the general practice history, and can in that sense be relied upon (like all other practice of an international organization) for interpreting the agreement. As discussed earlier, the question is then whether the practice is sufficient to 'establish agreement' of the parties to the interpretation involved. There seems to be some tendency in GATT to accept panel reports as fairly definitive practice in this regard.

There is, however, an even more formidable possibility regarding the effect of panel reports. As discussed earlier, it is conceivable that the Contracting Parties under Article XXV have the power definitively to interpret the GATT, in the sense of adopting a resolution of interpretation which binds all parties to the GATT, even those that voted against the resolution. Thus, it could be argued that the Contracting Parties' adoption of a panel report is such definitive interpretation. If this were the case, the effect of the panel reports would be even stronger than precedent. They would be the equivalent of a resolution of interpretation formally adopted by the Contracting Parties, and would bind all Contracting Parties for the future, at least until they adopted a contrary or inconsistent resolution of interpretation.

The problem at this point is whether the Contracting Parties, when they adopt a panel report, intend it to be a definitive interpretation on their part. I suggest that they do not. I believe it is most likely that, if asked, representatives of Contracting Parties would indicate that they intended no such formidable result for their adoption of a panel report. Indeed, many of them (not being trained in the law) would be somewhat frightened by the question.

6.3 National government procedures for GATT disputes

(a) The United States and its section 301 procedures

Under traditional international law doctrines, nations are almost the only 'subjects' of international law, and international procedures are open only to nation-states and in some cases to international organizations. This is generally true today, although there is a developing body of practice and thought that permits individuals as well as business firms to be subjects. Nevertheless, the primary international law procedures for dispute settlement, such as the World Court, are available only to nation-states or international organizations. When individuals have a complaint against some foreign nation, the traditional approach requires those individuals to get their own governments to raise the matter in international diplomatic processes or tribunals. This is called 'diplomatic protection'.[46]

Under traditional practice of diplomatic protection, the nation whose citizen has urged it to take up his or her cause is the 'owner' or controller of the case. If that nation refuses to proceed, the individual usually has no recourse under international law. That nation's domestic law may give the individual some recourse, as happens with laws regarding the taking of property, but under international law the national government officials have the final say as to whether to bring a citizen's complaint to the attention of an offending nation or to an international proceeding. The theory supposedly is that national policy may make it more important for a nation to refrain from pursuing its citizen's problems in some cases. Good relations with a more powerful state may lead a small nation to refrain from aggravating the powerful state by raising with it the complaints of a few of its citizens.

The traditional approach for a US citizen who has a complaint against actions taken by a foreign nation is to bring that complaint to the attention of the US government (usually the Department of State), and try to get the US government to intervene on behalf of the citizen with the foreign authorities. This applies in cases of foreign economic matters, such as when a foreign nation expropriates property of an American citizen. It applies also when a foreign nation violates an international treaty obligation which would otherwise protect the economic or trade interests of an American citizen or firm. Thus, if a foreign country imposes a tariff which exceeds the limit set in its GATT obligations on imports from an American firm, the American firm will probably not find help in the courts of that foreign nation, and certainly cannot itself go directly to the GATT about the matter. It has to persuade the US government to take the matter up at GATT.

Dissatisfaction with the US government's handling of such complaints led the Congress to insert into the 1962 Trade Expansion Act a provision[47] which explicitly granted to the US President some authority to take retaliatory actions when foreign governments harmed the trade interests of American firms.[48]

In the 1974 Trade Act, section 301, the Congress revised this authority and set up a procedure which gave American firms and citizens the right formally to petition an agency of the US government, alleging that American commercial interests had been harmed by illegal or 'unfair' actions of foreign governments. This agency was charged with the responsibility of investigating the allegations, trying to get redress for the US citizen, and ultimately recommending various retaliatory actions to the President which were authorized by the statute. The 1979 Trade Agreements Act amended this law, as did the 1984 Tariff and Trade Act.

The more recent 1988 Omnibus Trade and Competitiveness Act also contains amendments to section 301. These have several objectives. Under certain circumstances the use of section 301 is to be more nearly 'mandatory', with executive branch discretion reduced in certain cases of 'unjustifiable' actions (for example, breach of legal obligations) by foreign governments. Certain exceptions are specified which restore some of the discretion, but overall Congress 'tightened' the 301 process and made it at least politically more difficult for the President's officials *not* to retaliate. This seems to be part of the source of rather bitter criticism of the 1988 Act coming from foreign government officials.[49]

Thus, today, the United States has a procedure which until 1984 was virtually unique in the world, under which US firms and citizens could petition the US government, in any case involving trade or commerce, to seek US government aid to redress any foreign-nation action which is deemed to be a violation of 'rights of the United States under any trade agreement' or which denies 'benefits to the United States under any trade agreement' or which is 'unjustifiable, unreasonable, or discriminatory and burdens or restricts United States commerce'.

The US section 301 procedures allow the government to 'self-initiate' a case, or a citizen to file a petition. If the case involves a trade agreement and no mutually acceptable resolution is obtained, the US must invoke the dispute settlement procedures of such agreement. Finally, the trade representative must (within certain time limits) make a published determination of what action the US should take. The statute delegates broad powers of response to the trade representative, including suspending or withdrawing trade agreement concessions, and imposing duties, fees or other restrictions on the offending country's trade. It makes clear that the procedure applies to trade in services as well as products, and allows responses either through MFN measures or discriminatory measures targeting the offending country.[50]

Several other features of the US procedure should be noted. Although required in some cases to use an international procedure, the US government is not obliged to abide by the outcome of such procedure, and in some cases does not even need to refrain from action until the international procedures are formally completed. This reflects considerable congressional dissatisfaction with the GATT dispute procedures.[51]

Furthermore, a section 301 case need not depend on foreign actions which violate international rules (which the statute usually terms 'unjustifiable') but may also be based on the statutory criteria of 'unreasonableness', and this gives the US much latitude unilaterally to define practices it deems to be unfair and deserving countermeasures.[52]

Finally, section 301 does not have an 'injury requirement' but, for practices not in violation of a trade agreement, requires the approximate equivalent: something which 'burdens or restricts United States commerce'.[53]

From the 1974 enactment of section 301 until June 1989 there have been at least 78 petitions accepted by the Office of the US Trade Representative. Of these, 20 concerned practices of the EC, while four more concerned actions of the EC member states. Eleven cases involved trade in services rather than goods, and two concerned the protection of intellectual property.

As the draughtsmen of section 301 foresaw, the utility of the procedure does not result from the counter action alone, but from the negotiation process assisted by the potential of counter action.[54]

Particularly in the light of recent US unilateral 'retaliations',[55] some of which were influenced by congressional sentiments expressed in the development of the Trade Act of 1988, it has been asked whether the US procedure is consistent with its GATT obligations. This question cannot easily be answered.

The usual starting-point of an analysis to answer that question is the notion that the mere existence of legislation or procedures which might result in a concrete action that violates a treaty, is normally not itself a treaty violation. The concrete action is usually necessary to establish the international law violation, unless of course the international rules expressly or impliedly impose an obligation on the nature of the legislation or procedure. For example, the international rule might explicitly state that parties to it must bring their legislation into conformity with some norm. That is not the case with the GATT rules here considered. Thus, unless there is an 'implied' rule of this type, perhaps partly implied by an obligation of 'good faith' in treaty relations, it is difficult to fault the US statutes or procedures as violating existing GATT norms. Of course, certain *actions* actually taken by the US under its law and procedure can (and do) violate GATT obligations.

The Uruguay Round negotiators seem aware of the threat to the integrity and system of GATT implied by certain US actions, and some have expressed the view that the negotiations must address and restrain such unilateralism.

(b) The 'new commercial policy instrument' of the EEC

In 1984 the EEC adopted a regulation on 'the strengthening of the common commercial policy with regard in particular to protection against illicit commercial practices'.[56] This regulation is designed to give individuals or firms in the EC the right to petition the EC Commission to begin an investigation of foreign government practices which are harming EC trade, and possibly to take action to counter those practices. The regulation seems to have been partly inspired by the US section 301 procedure, but as adopted it has some significant differences. In addition, it would be a mistake to assume that the same motivations were behind the EEC regulation as behind the US law. The EEC regulation is set in a very different governmental context and arguably has an important effect of altering the balance or allocation of power between EC institutions. For example, before the new regulation came into force, the only way in which the EC could act against unfair foreign practices was laid down by the 'Luxembourg Compromise', which effectively required a proposal of the Commission to be accepted by the Council without objection.[57] This meant that a member state government with a liberal trade position could 'veto' such reaction. Under the new regulation, once certain procedures are followed, a Commission proposal to take counter action cannot be as easily overturned in the Council by a member state. In the debate leading to its adoption, it was argued that this aspect of the regulation would help some governments (such as the French) – which traditionally were able to influence the Commission – in bringing about the adoption of trade-restricting measures.

In addition the balance of powers within the EC was altered by this regulation in several other ways. For example, the Commission is now authorized to launch a GATT dispute settlement procedure (subject to a 'guillotine' vote of the Council), whereas previously this required an affirmative decision by the Council.

Several interesting differences between the EEC regulation and the US section 301 law exist. First, under the regulation an international proceeding, if applicable, must always be invoked and followed through to its conclusion before the contemplated counter actions can be utilized.

Secondly, the regulation provides that it 'shall not apply in cases covered by other existing rules in the commercial policy field'.[58] This seems to suggest, for example, that anti-dumping and subsidization cases are more appropriately brought under other regulations relating to those actions.

Finally, it has been said:

> [T]he shift in emphasis from inward-looking protective measures to export promotion which has come to be identified with Section 301 is not reflected in the EEC instrument. Reg. No. 2641/84 primarily seeks to protect the Common Market against foreign unfair trade practices. Securing access to export markets for Community industries clearly has been a secondary objective in drafting the regulation.[59]

In fact, the several cases brought under the regulation have been directed at practices which affect EC exports.[60]

Obviously the US and EC developments raise the question of whether they represent a trend toward more formalistic procedures available to private individuals or firms in connection with the application and enforcement of international trade rules, at least under GATT and associated agreements. This will be discussed in the next section.

6.4 Reform of the dispute procedures

There has, as we have seen, been considerable comment about the weaknesses of the GATT dispute settlement processes, and much mention of the necessity of trying to improve these as one of the tasks of a new round of negotiation.[61] Clearly there are many obstacles to any serious reform, not the least of which is the fundamental disagreement on the policy and goals of the procedure, outlined in the first section of this chapter. Nevertheless, since so much attention is being directed to the question, it is not out of place to speculate a little on what types of further reforms might be desirable.

A valid and improved system[62] should encourage and assist settlement by the disputants, but it should encourage that settlement primarily by reference to the existing agreed rules rather than simply by reference to the relative economic or other power which the disputants possess. The mechanism should be designed so that as time goes on, greater confidence will be placed in the system, so that it will be more often used, and so that greater responsibilities can gradually be put upon it.

In order to establish that the dispute settlement mechanism relies primarily on reference to rules and their application, the fulcrum of a mechanism should be the opportunity to obtain an impartial and trusted decision on the interpretation or application of a previously agreed rule. To avoid tainting the process of that judgment, the impartial third-party decision of rule interpretations or application should be (as it most often is in the various legal systems of the world) relatively isolated from other processes such as the process of assisting in negotiation for settlement, or the process of rule formulation.

One possible framework for an improved dispute settlement procedure is a five-part approach (not dramatically different from what now exists in GATT) which can be outlined as follows:[63]

1. Bilateral consultations between the disputing parties without outside presence (as now provided).
2. Conciliation process, with the assistance of trained persons, probably from the secretariat, to assist the parties in resolving their dispute.
3. Panel and rulings: Similar to the current procedure, but with more emphasis on the impartiality of the panel members, use of a broader cadre for panels, and a separation of the conciliation process from the panel process. A goal is to increase the integrity and credibility of the 'findings', so these can have greater moral force (even without the use of sanctions). The panel report should therefore *always* be published quickly.
4. Policy body approval: As in the present procedure, a panel ruling would be submitted to the highest policy body, such as the GATT CONTRACTING PARTIES, for approval. This allows some flexibility for special circumstances or the recognition of the need for a new rule. The procedure should not allow either disputant to block approval of the panel report, and it should be recognized that the

policy body considerations go beyond the strict rules or the law, invoking for example 'equitable' principles.[64] Over time, the persuasiveness of the panel report and the credibility of the panel process would obviously have a great impact on the policy body's consideration of the panel reports.

5. Sanctions, such as suspending GATT concessions as now provided. History suggests that sanctions have limited use and that the international community is generally unwilling to accept or strengthen them. Thus at present, the system may well be best operated without sanctions.

Making progress in a body of 97 or more nations is always difficult, and while recognizing the divergence of opinion regarding dispute settlement procedures even between the EC and the US, it may be necessary to turn to methods of evolving a better procedure other than full GATT participation. In short a 'mini-lateral' approach[65] may be useful, allowing a small group of nations to develop an improved procedure to use in disputes among themselves, keeping the door open for other nations to join these procedures as time goes on. The developments of 'alternative and optional routes' available to parties which agree to them (such as the arbitration possibility included in the 1988 Montreal document) would be consistent with this approach.

Bilateral approaches are also an important option, although they worry some who feel they may undermine the multilateral system. The 1988 Free Trade Agreement between Canada and the United States has several far-reaching bilateral dispute settlement provisions which cover many GATT subjects also dealt with in the bilateral agreement.

One of these provisions created an international panel procedure which not only substitutes for appeal to domestic courts in anti-dumping and countervailing duty cases in the two countries, but is empowered to issue a decision which becomes directly applicable in the domestic law of the country concerned so as to bind the administration there.[66]

At some point in the future (it cannot happen soon), the participants in the international multilateral trade system might consider an approach to disputes and rule application that allows some modified means of direct access to procedures by individuals and private firms, perhaps after an appropriate international 'filter' to prevent spurious complaints. As my co-authors and I wrote in 1984:

> There are some interesting potentials in these precedents for the GATT and the international economic system, although they will probably not be readily accepted by the governments that participate in the GATT. But governments and business firms do desire greater predictability of national government economic actions in an increasingly interdependent world, and do desire greater balance and equality in actual implementation of negotiated international rules on economic matters. Those factors could lead governments to be willing to accept some sort of a mechanism by which individual citizens or firms could appeal directly to an international body like the GATT to determine whether a government obligated under the GATT or one of its codes has taken an action that is inconsistent with its international obligations.
>
> .   .   .   .
>
> Clearly, the typical governmental reluctance to relinquish any power or to constrain its field of discretion would discourage a move in the direction of the procedures described. On the other hand, it should be recognized that there are some advantages for governments in such a procedure. For one thing, if it were carefully designed and became reliable, governments might well find that the procedure would tend to de-emphasize and depoliticize many relatively minor trade or economic complaints that now exist between nations. For example, let us assume that Mr. A, a citizen in country A, finds that his exports to country B are being restrained improperly by country B, inconsistent with country B's international obligations. Under the current procedure, Mr. A must go to his own national government and get it to take up his matter with the foreign government. Thus, his case has immediately been raised to a diplomatic level. That quite often means, by the nature of things, that it has been raised to a fairly high level of official attention and consequently of public perception. On the other hand, if an appropriate international procedure existed, when Mr. A came to his government to complain about country B, country A officials

could refer Mr. A to that procedure and encourage him to use it, without taking any stand on the matter. It is quite possible that the issue could then be handled more expeditiously and routinely. The case would continue to be Mr. A's case, and not become country A's case. The issue would be Mr. A versus country B, instead of Mr. A and country A versus country B.

It is the view of at least one of the authors of this book that in all probability, early versions of such a procedure would have to allow the individual governments to exercise some kind of right of veto over their own citizens' attempts to invoke the process. However, this right could be accorded to national governments as a way to make them more comfortable with experimenting with the procedure, and could be designed to gradually die out (at least for all but the most exceptional cases).[67]

Once again we need to return to the dichotomy of policy pointed out in the first section of this chapter. A European author, in a book quoted approvingly by a major European diplomat, suggests that international resolution of disputes, at least regarding economic matters, has as its prime objective neither the ascertainment of right or wrong nor the establishment of responsibility, but instead the most rapid cessation of the violations.[68] That author, and others,[69] stress the importance of diplomatic means and negotiating approaches to resolving disputes.

Unfortunately, these viewpoints miss important policy considerations, and are often misleading. In the first place, it is useful to identify (or threaten to do so) the wrongdoer in an international dispute, especially if there is widespread acceptance of the validity of the process which determines this. But more important, it must be recognized that in most cases it is *not* the resolution of the specific dispute under consideration which matters most. Rather it is the efficient and just future functioning of the overall system which is the prime goal of a dispute settlement procedure. Thus it may be more important to clarify and provide predictive guidance about the application of a rule than to see that a 'judgment' be acceptable to either or both parties to the immediate dispute. Indeed, in some GATT proceedings, contracting parties other than the disputants have expressed a strong interest in a dispute process because the resulting precedent effect of a panel ruling could affect them.[70] If the policies of a 'rule-oriented diplomacy' (discussed earlier) make sense, they also tend to suggest a broader goal than the settlement of a particular dispute to the satisfaction of the disputants. Interesting evidence of the desire of important economic groups to support this broader goal is the urge of the 'intellectual property' groups to bring the IP issues into GATT. One of their stated reasons for this is the aim of applying the 'more rigorous' GATT dispute settlement procedures to the IP rules, so as to offer a better chance that those rules will be followed.

These questions are not absolute 'either/or' ones, however. If a rule is applied too rigidly, as a matter of routine, that too will damage the broader international trading system. On the other hand, excessive concern for diplomatic approaches designed to obscure or paper over differences will have its costs also.

Finally, there are other mechanisms and techniques for improving the 'rule integrity' of the GATT trade system. One approach, often termed 'surveillance', is to have committees or working groups systematically examine the trade measures of particular countries (perhaps on a rotation basis) and comment on the appropriateness of such measures to GATT policy.[71] Another is for a GATT body to report biannually (as has been done) on the status of the trading system, to flag discrepancies between measures actually taken (such as 'grey area' or export restraint arrangements)[72] and GATT rules, or to raise questions about the policy appropriateness of such measures.

The mid-term review agreements of December 1988 and April 1989 established a 'trade policy review mechanism' which is modelled to some extent on procedures followed in the OECD. This mechanism is one of the products of the Uruguay Round negotiating group on the 'functioning of the GATT system' and it is regarded by some as a significant development for the GATT. The basic idea is that there will be a regular schedule of trade policy reviews, to be carried out by the GATT Council at special meetings. Each of these reviews will focus on a particular country. Some countries will, because of their size and importance, be reviewed more frequently than others. The initial schedule established that the United States, Australia,[73] and Morocco will be the first Contracting Parties subject to review.

These reviews could indeed be an important addition to the

GATT, providing information to many GATT members about the trade policies of particular Contracting Parties, and offering an opportunity for criticism of those policies. However, it must be recognized that these reviews are not likely to have a significant impact on the implementation or effectiveness of the legal obligations contained in the variety of GATT treaties and protocols, including those that will come into effect at the end of the Uruguay Round. Indeed there are some risks that this review mechanism will divert attention from the legal norms in such a way as actually to decrease the pressure on Contracting Parties to observe those norms. To some degree, the trade policy review mechanism is a concession to the view that GATT is primarily a 'negotiating' or 'consulting' organization, rather than one which tries to define and implement reasonably precise norms to help the standardization of world trading activities.

7

MEMBERSHIP: SELECTIVE OR UNIVERSAL APPROACH?

7.1 Membership and the goals of GATT

In Chapter 3 we explored the current membership of GATT, noting the increase from the original 23 to the current 97. In addition, there are approximately 12 nations which have applied for GATT membership or indicated a desire to do so. The application of China, and the potential application of the USSR, of course, will have very great consequences for some of the fundamental principles of GATT.

It has been asked whether the GATT system should be designed to accommodate all countries that come to it with good intentions and peaceful objectives, or whether it should accommodate only those that have a certain viewpoint with respect to key economic policies. That is to say, should the international institution for trade and economic matters be limited to governments which generally pursue a 'market-oriented' economic system?

At the time of drafting the ITO charter the view was that the ITO would be a 'universal organization', somehow accommodating widely different views of economic structure. However, a number of the provisions in the ITO draft charter were certainly oriented more towards 'market economics' than otherwise, and this led some nations rather bitterly to oppose that draft charter.

With respect to the GATT itself, however, the countries involved in its drafting were pursuing a goal of reducing tariffs in the context of the advice of economists who favoured 'liberal trade' and market-oriented economies. The GATT text did not differ substantially in this respect from the comparable chapter in the ITO charter. Nevertheless, the GATT was perceived as a place where like-minded economies could accommodate their need to pursue liberal or open trade policies consistent with market-oriented governments.

Since the GATT had to fill the gap left by the failure of the ITO to materialize, the GATT gradually began to accommodate a much broader set of views with respect to market structure. It has accepted not only countries with markedly different levels of industrial development, but also countries with dramatically different viewpoints with respect to structuring economics. For example, the GATT currently has as Contracting Parties about six or seven countries that are generally considered to have 'non-market' or 'state-trading' structures.[1] Likewise, it has as members countries that are poor and whose governments pursue coordinated policies of economic development, in some cases very different from the market-oriented principles that motivate the governments of other GATT CPs.

Although the GATT has a number of non-market economies participating in it, these economies are relatively small. The structure for their participation differs from one to another, and these various structures reflect considerable perplexity on the part of GATT and these parties as to how to bring a state-trading nation into the GATT when the rules of GATT do not really provide for this. However, since the existing contracting parties of this type in GATT are relatively small, the GATT has been able uneasily to compromise and accommodate them without undue strain.[2]

Now the situation is changing. China is negotiating for re-entry, and the USSR too has raised the issue of its participation. These countries are large, their economies are very substantial, and therefore their participation in GATT will surely test many of the GATT rules and principles. Thus, the issue is raised as to whether the GATT should remain (or 'revert' to being) a forum designed primarily for market-oriented economies, or whether it should try to accommodate even large state-trading countries. The latter approach would require some fundamental rethinking about the role of GATT, and perhaps a substantial elaboration of a new set of rules to 'interface' between the market economies of GATT and the state-trading countries.

I feel that the GATT, or some structure related to it, should be designed to be 'universal' in orientation, and thus to accommodate all types of economies. One of the reasons for this goes back to the fundamental notion of the Bretton Woods system, i.e., the prevention of war, which in the economic context means embracing and establishing an institutional structure by which at least major powers of the world can try to iron out their differences. This fundamental goal means that there must be available some kind of an international institution for trade and all other economic endeavours, which will minimize the tensions and conflicts that inevitably arise even among nations whose economies are reasonably similar. (For example, notice the tensions occurring between the United States and Japan, both of which regard themselves as market-oriented economies.) This approach implies future GATT membership for the USSR. There are a number of specific measures that should be elaborated to facilitate this. If the countries concerned are to be integrated directly into GATT, and that certainly seems to be contemplated for China, then such elaboration of new rules will be necessary unless the GATT system is to be weakened.

7.2 The interface theory of managing economic relations

The stark reality of international economic relations is the accelerated development of interdependence, by which is meant that various economies in the world relate to one another to an increasing extent in such a way that economic forces, or conditions that develop in one economy, are transmitted rapidly to others. As already mentioned, this poses considerable difficulties for national leaders, who find it harder to satisfy the needs of their constituencies. National governments and governmental leaders feel vulnerable. The solution is to look towards an international approach, hopefully on agreed principles. But there are a number of different possibilities for such principles, possibilities about what we might call 'techniques to manage interdependence'. Three main alternatives come to mind:

(1) Harmonization: A system that gradually induces nations towards uniform approaches to a variety of economic regulations and structures. An example would be standardization of certain product specifications. An obvious difficulty would be the resistance of national or other groups which desire to main-

83

tain their particular individuality or contrary preference choices in structuring their economies.

✳ (2) Reciprocity: A system of continuous 'trades' or 'swaps' of measures to liberalize (or restrict) trade. GATT tariff negotiations have followed this approach, and there have been many variations on the 'reciprocity ideas'.

(3) The interface principle: This approach recognizes that different economic systems will always exist in the world, and tries to create the institutional means to ameliorate international tensions caused by those differences, perhaps through buffering or escape-clause mechanisms.

Obviously countries as different as China and the United States, or the Soviet Union and the EEC, will experience difficulties in developing an appropriate set of principles for their trade – principles that will satisfy their various citizens or constituents that such trade is fair to all concerned.

If what is needed is a broad concept of 'interface accommodation' among differing economic systems, even in countries as similar as, say, the United States and Japan, it can be argued that a parallel basic approach is needed for countries with a state-trading, or 'non-market' orientation, if those countries are to be accommodated in GATT. Reiterating what I have said earlier in this chapter, it should be noted that there are powerful reasons why such accommodation should be managed. Thus, the interface technique becomes very important.

7.3 Principles for state-trading or non-market economies

For the reasons already outlined, it will be tempting for the existing GATT nations to welcome China as a new member, and possibly later the Soviet Union. A risk of these impulses, however, is that the GATT will accept China and others without adequately thinking through the rules which would provide the appropriate 'interface' between those economies and the more market-oriented nations in GATT. These principles will be very important to the long-run viability of the GATT as a disciplining factor on potential members who are inclined to favour trade restrictions. Much detail will be needed in the treaty text to establish an interface mechanism, and the rules enunciated in such text will appear untidy, and indeed may annoy those who are 'free-market' purists and who wish to avoid any 'quantitative restrictions' or other alternative to free trade. However, the establishment of the interface mechanism is essential to avoid the danger of undermining the GATT.

In general there are three categories of problems that have to be explored and treated by an interface text:

(1) The problem of exports from the non-market economy (NME) to the GATT market economy contracting party.

(2) The problem of exports from the GATT market economy CP to the NME.

(3) The problem of competition between the GATT market economy CP and the NME in third markets.

For each category a fairly detailed text will be necessary, sometimes influenced by experiences of GATT with smaller NMEs, but recognizing necessary differences due to the size and importance of the applicant. Such a text could be part of the Protocol of Accession, or it could be a broader 'code' or even an amendment to GATT. Making this text part of the Protocol of Accession, however, is probably the simplest and most efficient way to proceed.

The first category, for example, raises the issue of the 'escape clause' or 'safeguards', as well as problems of 'unfair trade' such as dumping or subsidies. The application of anti-dumping or anti-subsidy duties to products from state-trading countries has been particularly troublesome.[3] Likewise an important and controversial issue has been the possibility of 'selective safeguards' (on a non-MFN basis) imposed on such products.

One approach in the discussions and negotiations currently under way is for the existing GATT countries to tell the NME applicant that it must become more market-oriented before it can be accepted into GATT. An alternative is to provide a gradual admission to GATT.

Both of these alternatives miss the essential point of a GATT 'interface principle'. It is not the purpose or role of the GATT to apply pressures on sovereign nations to accept market-oriented economic principles. The internal structure of a country's market should be left to that country's own judgment, as long as its practices do not harm other countries. The challenge to the GATT should be to enable such a country to participate meaningfully in the world

85

trading system, without doing harm either to that system or to other countries. The aim, therefore, should perhaps be to design a set of interface rules by which the applicant non-market economy can trade with the existing GATT market economies to the most feasible extent.

A better approach would be to structure the admission of such an applicant country on a 'two-track basis'. The first track would be admittance of the country on a full basis to all the usual rules of GATT without any special rules. By the second track, treaty terms would permit the GATT market economy to establish in its own national rules a provision that would allow its own producers to complain to a governmental body when they felt that imports from a non-market economy were causing them injury of a certain level. The complaint would have to specify why the particular products were alleged to be from a non-market or state-trading sector of the exporting country. That would have to be established by proofs and discussion, and decided by the national government agency.

Once it was decided that the imported products were indeed from a non-market or state-trading sector, the second track would prevail, and this would provide for an immediate injury test with some agreed threshold (e.g. 'material injury'). If that threshold were established by the importing country's agency, then those goods would be charged a duty (tariff) equal to the difference between the importing price and some 'bench-mark price'. It would be understood that these procedures would substitute both for the escape clause, or 'fair-trade' case, and for dumping and countervailing duty proceedings and other 'unfair-trade' laws.

The key would be to define the level of the 'bench-mark price'. This has been much discussed in the US Congress. One reasonably attractive approach is to set the bench-mark at the average price of the imports of the like product from that market economy which ships substantial amounts of the goods, and has the lowest price for those goods. This would seem to be the most generous in allowing the competition from the non-market economy, and yet would provide a bench-mark to give some assurance to the importing country's domestic producers that the non-market economy's state-traded goods would not be 'unfairly' low-priced.

This would be a selective approach, that is, not on an MFN basis. It would be analogous to selective safeguards (which some non-market officials view as anathema, but will probably be necessary).

The quid pro quo for the non-market economy in accepting such a 'second track', apart from membership of the GATT, would be greater international discipline on the selective bench-mark provision. Thus, the measures could be limited in duration and also limited as to the type of injury test that would be required (possibly with some threshold quantitative criteria).

In addition, as part of all this, there would be a GATT working party, meeting periodically to explore the problems and tensions arising between the state-trading country and the GATT. This would be a two-way discussion, exploring the policies of the GATT NME member, and also accommodating that member's complaints against other GATT members. Such a body might also play a role in reviewing some of the national governments' second-track decisions, such as the injury test or the decision that a particular sector was state-trading and non-market oriented.

The advantage of a two-track approach is that it is relatively self-adjusting to the extent of market-economy principles followed in the new NME. It is not based on a policy of GATT pressure to marketize the economy. The applicant nation is left free to decide for itself what its system will be, recognizing that state-trading structures will come under the second-track rules. If, over time, a greater portion of that country's economy becomes 'market-oriented' it will automatically, without a timetable or tortured international determination, become increasingly eligible for normal GATT rules under the first track. It is a gradualist approach, yet imposing disciplines on the existing GATT nations' tendencies to use special measures for excluding products from non-market economies.

One can see from this fairly elaborate description that negotiation of these interface principles will not be easy. There are a number of intricacies that I have not dealt with. Furthermore, I have left open the two additional areas of concern: exports to the non-market economy and competition in third markets. These areas also would require considerable thought and development of fairly elaborate and perhaps untidy interface treaty texts.

PART III

A New Constitution

for World Trade?

8

REFORMING THE GATT SYSTEM

8.1 Thinking longer term

Any attempt to improve the GATT system and to try to correct some of the various problems identified with that system can obviously take several different approaches. One approach would be a step by step approach, to remedy a few problems at a time and spread this effort out over a number of years. This has much appeal since easier issues can be taken up first, and there is less chance of opposition than might be the case with a broader approach. On the other hand, the piecemeal approach makes it harder to develop tradeoffs which can attract a coalition of constituencies (the basic rationale for large negotiating rounds), and often takes so long that the 'reform' runs out of steam well before completion of the task.

The current negotiation in the 'FOGS' group seems to take a very cautious approach. Perhaps this is realistic and pragmatic, that is, as much as can be expected. Yet there are some converging trends in the GATT system which might suggest that there is some chance for a more fundamental reform. Here is a partial list:

(1) The Uruguay Round is vast and complex, and addresses several important 'new issues', particularly services, intellectual property, and trade-related investment measures. It is unclear how some of the results of negotiations on these issues can be incorporated into the GATT system. Thus a certain amount of thinking about the 'institutional structure' will be necessary to prepare for the end of the Uruguay Round.

(2) There appears to be growing concern about the relationship of some of the Tokyo Round codes to the GATT system.

(3) The admittance of some new or potential new members (such as China) will require consideration of how the GATT system can embrace large economies structured on the basis of principles other than market economics.

(4) There is much concern about the dispute settlement process, and at least some recognition that the 'reforms' so far raised in the negotiation are relatively timid.

(5) Many other problems of the weak constitutional structure of the GATT system have been increasingly recognized.

(6) The world economy is changing at an increasingly rapid pace, and the GATT system is relatively rigid, making it difficult to adapt it to many of the changes likely to occur. Thus it can be argued that a better 'constitution' will be needed for the next decades or next century, to address a large number of 'new issues'.

(7) National governments recognize that an international structure of rules and obligations can be useful in seeking change at home.

(8) World economic relations have changed dramatically in recent decades. Changes include growing 'interdependence' and speed of communication, impact of economic circumstances on other countries, risky 'unilateral' actions by major trading nations, and the inability of the traditional GATT system rules effectively to address a series of new trading problems or structures.

Even the convergence of all these forces, however, may not be sufficient to overcome a variety of negative conservative political forces, including those of special interests which feel that 'national sovereignty' enables them to exert their influence on world events, at least when that influence is aimed at preventing change and when international 'consensus' rules give key governments the power to block international changes.

Whether or not it is likely that a broader or more fundamental set of recommendations will be implemented in the next few years, there may be some value in proposing such recommendations. They can form a checklist of possibilities, some of which can then be taken up independently. By setting these recommendations in the framework of an overall fundamental approach, potential inconsistencies in different recommendations can be thought through. Likewise, the longer-term implications of the individual recommendations can often be better understood in the context of overall approaches.

Finally, it should be recognized that similar exercises regarding fundamental changes in human institutions have sometimes made substantial contributions to such changes. The Spinelli Commission of the European Parliament undertook a broad exercise to draft a new 'constitution' for the European Communities, a task completed in 1984 with the adoption of a report by the European Parliament.[1] This effort included a prototype draft treaty drawn up by a group of legal scholars. Although this draft treaty was not completely accepted, it nevertheless had an obvious effect on the governmental processes leading to the EC Single Act which came into force on 1 July 1987 and has had a major influence on the EC, its restructuring, and its goal of a unified market in 1992.

Likewise, in the United States there are several legal organizations (including the American Law Institute and the Commissioners of Uniform Laws)[2] which sometimes undertake major drafting exercises resulting in proposed federal or state statutes. These draft laws sometimes have a very important effect on subsequent changes in the actual laws.

Thus, in the next part of this chapter I propose to suggest, as an exercise pursuing the possibilities mentioned above, the outlines of a fundamental restructuring of the GATT 'constitutional system', primarily in the form of a new draft 'charter' for a World Trade Organization. Improbable as this may sound, I suggest that the thinking process it requires, and the thinking it may stimulate, can have a longer-term constructive influence on world economic cooperation. The next step would be to constitute an unofficial and academic 'drafting/advisory' group which could try its hand at putting these and other ideas into concrete language, probably with a number of 'square brackets' or alternative suggestions. At least such an effort might further stimulate thought about some of the difficult institutional problems of the GATT system, which may otherwise be neglected.

8.2 A new charter for international trade cooperation

The hypothesis to be discussed here is that it would be an important step towards furthering world peace and economic well-being, pursuing the original goals of the GATT system, to establish a new simple treaty instrument which would explicitly create an overall organization for international commerce, focused on the institutional and procedural issues, largely leaving substantive rules and obligations to other treaty instruments such as the GATT which would be served and 'sheltered' by the broader organization. In developing outlines of such a treaty instrument I have not hesitated to draw upon a number of models including the 1955 draft OTC, and upon other writings including those concerning services trade[3] and GATT dispute settlement procedures.[4]

The basic thrust of the proposal is to have the new treaty instrument contain the organizational 'constitution' for an institution which could be variously named, but which I will call (for simplicity's sake) a World Trade Organization (WTO). Unlike the Havana Charter for an ITO, the WTO charter would not contain many substantive obligations. Those would continue to be expressed in the GATT (which should become 'definitive' rather than provisional) and a number of other 'codes' or agreements, all of which would be facilitated and served by the WTO structure.

This new treaty instrument could be part of a Uruguay Round Final Act, or one of the optional or required agreements listed in such a Final Act, or it could be separately considered after the Uruguay Round is completed. There would, however, be obvious advantages in including the WTO charter as part of the Uruguay Round results. If such were the case, the key countries could enter the 'end-game' negotiation of the Uruguay Round with the understanding that the other agreements of the Uruguay Round, including services and intellectual property, would be finalized in the light of the institutional setting of a WTO. Part of the final commitments would be an agreement on the part of a minimum number of key countries, including some developing countries, to accept the WTO as a condition of the coming into force of part or all of the Uruguay Round results. In addition, national procedures (especially the 'fast track' in the US) to implement those results would be available for necessary legislative approval.

The WTO charter would not only provide the institutional structure for GATT and many other agreements, but would perform the role of an institutional agreement for service trade agreements and service sector agreements.[5] Likewise it would define the relationship of an intellectual property 'code'.[6] It would explicitly recognize the duty of this organization to provide service for these and other 'new subjects' of the Uruguay Round and later negotiations.

The WTO would inherit the 'ICITO'[7] powers, property, and tasks as soon as the ICITO members approved. It would establish a 'centralized panel procedure' to play a role in the dispute settlement procedures of the GATT and all the side agreements (while reserving certain functions of that procedure to the various councils or committees of each of the other agreements). It would also establish some explicit guidelines for the relationship of other treaty instruments to the WTO. Finally, it would set up a smaller body to act as a more efficient guiding group for the organization, since the size of the GATT membership has now become such as to make such guidance difficult except through informal means which are sometimes resented.

An outline of the potential provisions for such a new 'charter' follows.

WTO Part I: Objectives and establishment

The first article in this part would set forth the objectives of the organization, using language of the preamble of the GATT and the Havana and OTC charter drafts.

Another article would 'establish' the organization, and suggest that it be a UN specialized agency and have legal status with privileges and immunities.

WTO Part II: Membership, organization, and functions

Article 3 would provide for membership, which would be open to all GATT contracting parties, parties to the other treaty instruments of the GATT system (including the EC), and to new members upon a specified vote.

Article 4 would establish requirements that members accept the obligations of certain affiliated treaties, including the GATT, except in special cases where a nation might be permitted membership on special terms. This could be a way to provide membership in the WTO, while establishing a special relationship for large economies with structures which do not fit well into GATT, such as a large non-market economy. As to other 'sheltered agreements', such as service-sector agreements, acceptance could be optional (except that groups of nations might among themselves have requirements based on reciprocity that all nations in a group accept specified agreements).

One objective would be a 'universal membership' principle that would allow the fullest feasible participation of all countries, subject to certain minimum obligations but not so extensive as to exclude countries or to admit them in a context where it is tacitly recognized that compliance with obligations is unlikely.

An important provision would be similar to GATT Article XXXV, which authorizes an 'opt-out' choice between two contracting parties. As established in GATT, this is available at one time only – at the time one or the other of the 'opt-out' pair enters the GATT for the first time. In fact, there have been situations in GATT which a later 'opt-out' might clarify.

Article 6 would outline a series of functions which the organization would undertake. These could include matters similar to Article 3 of the OTC draft charter: facilitate consultation, sponsor negotiations, collect and analyse data and information. In addition the new GATT surveillance mechanism outlined in the Montreal declaration could be included here. It should be made clear that the scope of attention of the organization would include 'new issues', both those of the Uruguay Round, and potential newer ones that will emerge.

WTO Part III: Structure and voting

The overall structure for the 'governance' of the organization would be spelled out, and might (like the OTC draft structure) include an 'assembly' of all members (one vote per member), plus a smaller 'executive council'. The latter would undoubtedly be a sensitive issue, but needs to be considered. The OTC draft provided for an executive committee of 17 members, elected by the assembly but always including the five most economically important members, and representatives from varying levels of development, types of economies, and geographical areas.

This structure tries hard to avoid the problems of the extremes of a system of one vote per nation, on the one hand, and a 'consensus system' that can result in a virtual veto or least-common-denominator approach, on the other hand. One way to do this is explicitly to recognize some effective economic power differences among nations (the IMF and World Bank use a weighted voting system), but to do so in a way that prevents the powerful from having 'unfair' influence. Without such recognition, however, major powers are unlikely to comply with certain actions or norms of a one vote per nation system, thus lending considerable instability to the overall system. An alternative would be an 'advisory council' which would not have voting authority, but would advise the director-general and the assembly.

For efficiency and economy, the assembly or sub-groups of the assembly should have separately enumerated powers with respect to various 'sheltered treaties'. For example, only assembly members who are also contracting parties of GATT should vote on certain GATT actions. The principle that all assembly members can discuss and observe during such actions would be an advantage to the 'openness and transparency' of the organization. However it might be necessary to allow governing bodies of the various sheltered treaties to meet separately for particular purposes.

In addition, a 'general council' (separate from the 'executive council') could be established along the lines of the current GATT Council, to meet frequently on many matters and act in place of the assembly, with right of appeal to the assembly.

The WTO charter might simply state that parties to 'sheltered treaties', including the GATT, can 'delegate' powers to the assembly or the WTO organization, specifying which assembly members can vote on which issues. An overriding control or even veto of the executive council would probably be necessary.

WTO Part IV: Secretariat and administration
The new 'charter' would clear up various administrative problems of the GATT, with explicit provisions for a secretariat, a director-general (with term and mode of selection), a budget, amounts of member contribution, etc. The provisions on member contributions should take account of the fact that different 'sheltered treaty instruments' have different sets of members.

WTO Part V: Centralized panel procedure and the dispute settlement process
A common, unified, panel procedure which would become a part of each of the various dispute settlement procedures of the 'sheltered treaties' as well as dealing with issues arising directly under the WTO would be an important feature of the new organization. (It is possible, as a fall back, to have a separate protocol of dispute settlement procedures, which would apply as an 'optional protocol' only to those which accept it. Reciprocity or 'code conditionality' (where only those who sign will receive the benefits) would be built into this. An even further fall back would allow nations (again

reciprocally negotiated) to apply the central procedure to specified obligations only.)

Earlier we discussed a proposal for a five-part dispute settlement procedure, which includes: (1) bilateral consultation; (2) mediation and conciliation with the aid of secretariat services; (3) an impartial panel finding or ruling; (4) a 'political filter' of acceptance by a representative political body; and (5) finally (and rarely) a sanction-ing process such as withdrawal of concessions. This approximates fairly closely to what has now evolved in GATT.

There is, however, a considerable problem with the multitude of different dispute procedures now provided in many 'codes'. Such a situation creates disputes about the appropriate forum, and con-fusion about the procedures and their complexity. This makes it more difficult for smaller countries to understand and use the procedure effectively. Thus, the new organization should set up a unified procedure. However, parties to sheltered treaties could retain in them all matters regarding the fourth and fifth steps mentioned above. The WTO chapter on disputes would set forth a common set of procedures for the first three steps, and this would go a long way to avoid 'forum shopping' and forum disputes. It would provide a common set of detailed procedures and allow the experience and evolution of those procedures to develop naturally and centrally, so that such experience would apply to all future disputes (avoiding 'reinventing the wheel' in each treaty procedure).

In addition, provisions should be made to clarify the legal obligations of parties to a dispute, and the effect of a panel ruling (after acceptance). One potentially explosive issue is whether the WTO procedure would explicitly allow retaliation through actions involving a different type of trade than that which was involved in the infraction. For example, would the charter provide an opportun-ity for product trade measures in response to breaches of service or intellectual property standards? Or vice versa?

I would also repeat[8] that it would be wise to eliminate the imprecise language of 'nullification or impairment' as a basis for a dispute settlement complaint. Rather, for relative (never perfect!) stability and predictability of the system, the focus should be upon agreed (treaty) obligations which bind the defending nation.

WTO Part VI: Some central substantive obligations
A core list of obligations (mostly procedural) might be considered

for the WTO charter. This could include general obligations to consult, to avoid action harming other nations, to abide by dispute settlement results, and to provide procedural fairness and 'transparency' in domestic actions affecting international economic relations. It is probably best not to include here certain key traditional obligations such as MFN, or national treatment, since new issues may need to apply these differently depending on the various subject matters involved.

A common 'waiver' provision might be established, which however could be excluded by explicit mention in a sheltered agreement. Likewise, there might be some 'unless otherwise specified' clauses, which would contain certain obligations that would apply in the context of all sheltered treaties unless such treaty (or its governing body) specified otherwise.

Finally, there might be included some common 'exceptions', such as 'national security', and 'general health' and police power exceptions. The advantage of having these in the charter instrument, even if they apply only 'unless otherwise specified', is that over time a body of practice and interpretations can develop more efficiently for clauses in a central charter than if variations of language and context must be considered for each of the many 'sheltered' agreements.

WTO Part VII: Sheltered treaty instruments
Careful thought and drafting are needed to provide for the WTO clauses which would establish the relationship of 'sheltered treaties' (including the GATT) to the WTO. An annexe list of current agreements permitted to be so sheltered should be included. Then an article should specify certain conditions for adding to this annexe. One condition should be that the agreement be open for membership to all nations which are WTO members and which are willing and able to accept the obligations of the agreement in good faith. Another condition would be that the WTO central dispute procedure (steps (1), (2) and (3)) would apply to all sheltered agreements. Finally, the 'unless otherwise specified' clauses of part VI would apply to all sheltered agreements.

WTO Part VIII: Final provisions
An article regarding amendments is obviously necessary, and should steer clear of some of the difficulties of the comparable article in GATT, i.e. it should avoid too high an acceptance requirement, and

make any amendment applicable to all members once adopted, even those who voted against it. The WTO structure would allow amendment requirements that would involve the executive council as well as the assembly. For example, an amendment could require an affirmative majority vote of both the assembly and the executive council, and subsequent acceptance by a majority of all members including a two-thirds majority of the council.

Other typical final provisions would follow, including entry into force, ratification and deposit, and UN registration. The WTO would be the repository for the charter and all sheltered agreements.

The provisions on coming into force could be structured at the end of the Uruguay Round to be part of an overall package of reciprocal benefits, so that an important core of nations must accept before entry into force. Indeed, it is possible that acceptance of the charter would be a necessary pre-condition for the application of some substantive Uruguay Round agreements.

8.3 Step by step

Except for those historically anomalous moments of extraordinary creativity regarding international institutions (such as at the end of World War II), governments and diplomats seem to prefer the least dramatic approaches feasible. As indicated at the outset of this chapter, a possible alternative approach to the restructuring of GATT (instead of pursuing the idea of a new 'charter') would be to think through a series of improvements and try to implement those on a step by step basis over a period of time. Obviously there are advantages and disadvantages for either approach. In this section, I want to explore somewhat the 'step-by-step' possibilities.

It should be remembered, however, that at the end of the Uruguay Round, the GATT Contracting Parties will necessarily face a series of important GATT institutional issues. Of course, even in that context, a 'step-by-step' approach could be taken, by which each of these problems would become the subject of a separate solution, albeit in the overall context of the conclusion of the Uruguay Round. These issues include at least the following:

(1) How will the results of the negotiation on trade in services be related to the GATT? Will services be integrated into the GATT in some way? Will they be served by the GATT secretariat?

(2) How will the results of the Uruguay Round negotiations on

intellectual property subjects be related to the GATT? What will be the relationship between GATT and the WIPO (World Intellectual Property Organization) with respect to those results?

(3) Will important new rules or norms developed in the Uruguay Round negotiation be implemented through amendments to GATT, or through separate treaty instruments like those of the MTN (Tokyo Round) codes? What will be the relationship of such codes to the GATT? What will be the possibilities for amending the GATT?

(4) The results of the agricultural negotiation will particularly pose the problem just mentioned, along with broader issues of how to reform the GATT structure so as meaningfully to implement the results of the agricultural negotiation.

(5) If China is admitted to the GATT (as is highly likely), what measures will be concluded during the Uruguay Round (or after) to 'interface' the Chinese state-trading system into the GATT?

(6) What improvements will be made in the dispute settlement procedures?

(7) What can be done about the inclination of some major powers to take 'unilateral actions', sometimes arguing for retaliation against practices of other nations?

(8) What further changes can be made concerning the relationship of the Tokyo Round codes to the GATT?

In addition to the above subjects, almost all of which will certainly require attention, there are some other issues which *should* require attention by the end of the Uruguay Round or soon thereafter, including:

(1) What about future rounds? What about future negotiations with respect to other service sectors?

(2) What about an appropriate arrangement for incorporating the Soviet Union into the GATT system?

(3) How can the GATT handle its governance procedures as its membership numbers more than 100? Should there be a smaller governance group established? Should the CG18 (Consultative Group of 18 formed during the Tokyo Round) be enhanced? Should the focus be on an advisory group to advise the director-general, or on a governing structure with certain definitive delegated powers?

If in fact the GATT Contracting Parties are reasonably successful at the end of the Uruguay Round in solving a number of these issues, the aggregate of those issues will be (in all but name) a fundamental

101

new charter for the GATT. Nevertheless, some of the issues above may be separated from others, and Contracting Parties given certain options of how to proceed rather than facing an 'all-or-nothing' decision that would put everything together in one big final package.

However, there is always a likelihood that the Uruguay Round will not be quite so successful, and that certain parts of it will be held over for later negotiations. In addition, some of the above points could be elaborated or embellished by further activity during the next decade, in pursuance of a 'step-by-step' reform approach.

Finally, it must be recognized that there are some 'GATT reform issues' which probably do not have a particularly high priority and yet which could be taken up at some point, possibly after the Uruguay Round, with a view to reinforcing the GATT constitution. Two such issues come to mind:

(1) Phasing out the ICITO (Interim Commission for the ITO), and establishing explicit legal status for the GATT, as well as a secretariat, property holdings, and so on. This could stabilize the pension system for the GATT secretariat and clarify questions of privileges and immunities.

(2) The GATT could finally be applied 'definitively' instead of 'provisionally', and in particular grandfather rights could be abolished or transferred to some kind of protocol exception, with a phase-out schedule.

Conclusion

A quotation from the *Wall Street Journal* comes to mind:

> The key problem is that member nations, particularly the US, don't trust GATT's administrative machinery. . . . Instead there's a growing inclination for a do-it-yourself policy, a revival of unilateralism . . . .
> The GATT machinery has to be improved or replaced with something like the proposed International Trade Organization. The question is how to create confidence in the new pro-cedures.[9]

The old comfortable procedures of diplomacy among a small group of similar nations will no longer suffice for the GATT. A rule-oriented 'constitution' is evolving and is badly needed. A successful completion of the very ambitious Uruguay Round will only reinforce that need. (The proponents of an intellectual property agreement in GATT are among those who have made this quite clear.) In addition, such a successful completion will in fact require some fundamental changes in the GATT 'constitution'. The critical question is whether those changes will be carefully thought through or be merely the result of the happenstance of the negotiation endgame.

APPENDIX

List of GATT Contracting Parties and Council members as of 1 October 1989

Antigua & Barbuda
Argentina*
Australia*
Austria*
Bangladesh*
Barbados*
Belgium*
Belize
Benin
Bolivia
Botswana
Brazil*
Burkina Faso
Burundi
Cameroon*
Canada*
Central African
  Rep.*
Chad
Chile*
Colombia*
Congo*
Côte d'Ivoire*
Cuba*
Cyprus*
Czechoslovakia*
Denmark*
Dominican Republic*
Egypt*
Finland*
France*
Gabon*
Gambia

Germany, Fed.
  Rep. of*
Ghana*
Greece*
Guyana
Haiti
Hong Kong*
Hungary*
Iceland*
India*
Indonesia*
Ireland*
Israel*
Italy*
Jamaica*
Japan*
Kenya
Korea, Rep. of*
Kuwait*
Lesotho
Luxembourg*
Madagascar*
Malawi
Malaysia*
Maldives
Malta
Mauritania
Mauritius
Mexico*
Morocco*
Myanmar (Burma)*
Netherlands*
New Zealand*

Nicaragua*
Niger
Nigeria*
Norway*
Pakistan*
Peru*
Philippines*
Poland*
Portugal*
Romania*
Rwanda
Senegal*
Sierra Leone
Singapore*
South Africa*
Spain*
Sri Lanka*
Suriname
Sweden*
Switzerland*
Tanzania*
Thailand*
Togo
Trinidad & Tobago*
Turkey*
Uganda
United Kingdom*
United States*
Uruguay*
Yugoslavia*
Zaire*
Zambia
Zimbabwe*

*Contracting Parties which participate as members of the Council.
Number of Contracting Parties: 97.
Number of members of the GATT Council: 72 = 74%.

NOTES

Full publication details of the key works of reference will be found in the Select Bibliography. Such works are identified by abbreviated titles in the notes.

Chapter 1

1 See 1947 Protocol of Provisional Application, 55 UNTS 308; 30 October 1947, 61 Stat. pts. 5, 6 TIAS No. 1700.
2 See GATT Document GATT/LEG/1 and Supplements.
3 Details of these works are given in the Select Bibliography.
4 See Appendix.

Chapter 2

1 See Jackson, *World Trade and the Law of GATT* and Jackson, *World Trading System.*
2 See, for example, R.N. Cooper, 'Trade Policy as Foreign Policy', in R.M. Stern (ed.), *US Trade Policies in a Changing World Economy* (Cambridge MA: MIT, 1987), pp. 291–336.
3 See United Nations Monetary and Financial Conference (Bretton Woods, NH, 1–22 July 1944), Proceedings and Documents 941 (US Department of State Pub. No. 2866, 1948).
4 See *An Act to extend the Authority of the President under section 350 of the Tariff Act of 1930 as amended, and for other purposes*, 5 July 1945, Pub. L. 79–130, 59 Stat. 410.
5 1 UN ECOSOC Res. 13, UN Doc. E/22 (1946).

6 For example, if a tariff commitment for a maximum 10% tariff charge were made, a country might nevertheless decide to use a quantitative restriction to prevent imports and thus would evade the trade liberalizing effect of the tariff commitment.

7 See GATT, Article XXV, *Basic Instruments and Selected Documents*, vol. 4 (March 1969) and 55 UNTS 194. See also Jackson, *World Trade and the Law of GATT* and Jackson, *World Trading System*. The contracting parties are expressed in capital letters in the agreement when they are 'acting jointly'.

8 'Most-favoured nation' refers to an obligation found in a number of trade and other commercial treaties over several centuries. In GATT Article I this is worded as follows: 'With respect to customs duties and charges of any kind . . . and with respect to the method of levying such duties and charges, and with respect to all rules and formalities in connection with importation and exportation . . . any advantage, favor, privilege or immunity granted by any contracting party to any product originating in or destined for any other country shall be accorded immediately and unconditionally to the like product originating in or destined for the territories of all other contracting parties.'

The meaning of this clause can be summarized by saying that every country shall grant to a beneficiary of its MFN obligation, treatment or privileges at least as good as that which it grants to any other country. In short, it is a non-discrimination clause. See, for example: Jackson, *World Trading System*, Chapter 6; Jackson, *World Trade and the Law of GATT*, Chapter 11; 'Equality and Discrimination in International Economic Law (XI): The General Agreement on Tariffs and Trade', *The British Yearbook of World Affairs* (1983), 224.

Thus, a GATT Contracting Party which limits its tariff on an item imported from another country, must also so limit its tariffs on the same item imported from any GATT country.

9 See GATT, Article XXIX, and Jackson, *World Trade and the Law of GATT*, Section 2.4.

10 Jackson, *World Trading System*, p. 33.

11 Ibid., p. 34.

12 See above, note 4. The act expired on 12 June 1948.

13 See UN Doc. EPCT/TAC/4, 8 (1947).

14 See Jackson, *World Trade and the Law of GATT*, Section 3.3.

15 See Vermulst and Hansen, 'The GATT Protocol of Provisional Application: A Dying Grandfather?', *Columbia Journal of Transnational Law*, vol. 27 (1989), at p. 263.

16 See Jackson, *World Trading System*, Chapter 11.

17 See above, note 15.

18 See Jackson, *World Trade and the Law of GATT*, p. 154.
19 Ibid., Chapter 6.
20 GATT, BISD 14 Supp. 17 (1966).
21 See Jackson, *World Trade and the Law of GATT*, p. 51.
22 See Jackson, *World Trading System*, p. 38.

Chapter 3

1 Eighteen GATT contracting parties have no current GATT schedule. See GATT, *Status of Legal Instruments* (GATT: Geneva: looseleaf). Each of these members acceded under the Article XXVI:(5) (e) procedure. See Jackson, *World Trading System*.

2 See generally Jackson, *World Trade and the Law of GATT*, Section 4.6. It was felt that it would be unreasonable to force a nation to accept an agreement with another nation when it may have compelling political reasons not to enter into such a relationship with another country. As of 6 June 1988, 13 contracting parties were exercising such an option, see GATT L/6361 (1988).

3 See Jackson, *World Trade and the Law of GATT*, pp. 98–109.

4 All but three of the 1979 MTN arrangements had measures permitting non-application of the rights and obligations as between signatories. The three that contained no such waiver provision were the Arrangement Regarding Bovine Meat (GATT, BISD 26 Supp. 84 (1980)), the International Dairy Arrangement (GATT, BISD 26 Supp. 91 (1980)), and the Agreement on the Implementation of Article VII (GATT, BISD 26 Supp. 116 (1980)).

5 Among the original GATT 'members' were Southern Rhodesia (now Zimbabwe), Burma, and Ceylon (now Sri Lanka) even though at the time they were not independent nations.

6 See Jean Groux and Philippe Manin, *The European Communities in the International Order* (Brussels: European Commission, 1985), Pt II, Chapter 1; see also E.U. Petersmann, 'Participation of the European Communities in GATT: International Law and Community Law Aspects', in O'Keeffe and Schermers (eds.), *Mixed Agreements* (Boston: Kluwer, 1986), pp. 167–98, and 'The EEC as a GATT Member – Legal Conflicts between GATT Law and European Community Law', in Hilf, Jacobs and Petersmann (eds.), *The European Community and GATT* (Deventer: Kluwer, 1986), pp. 23–71.

7 See Chung-chou Li, 'Resumption of China's GATT Membership', *Journal of World Trade Law*, vol. 21 (1987), 25; Robert Herzstein, 'China and GATT: Legal and Policy Issues raised by China's participation in the General Agreement on Tariffs and Trade', *Law and Policy In International Business*, vol. 18 (1986), 371.

8 Special problems of China and GATT are discussed further in Chapter 7.

9 For example, Hong Kong has brought an action before a GATT Panel, although the request for the establishment of the Panel was placed by the UK. See GATT, BISD 30 Supp. 129 (1984).

10 See GATT/1384, 24 April 1986.

11 See Jackson, *World Trade and the Law of GATT*, Chapters 6 and 7. See also GATT, INF/236 (1987), List and Index of Documents Issued by Bodies (especially 'Index of Documents by Bodies' which lists the Committees of GATT).

12 See GATT Newsletter, No. 61, May 1989.

13 See for example *Department of State Bulletin*, vol. 86 (July 1986), 1; vol. 87 (August 1987), 1; *International Trade Reporter*, vol. 4 (1987), 784 on the Venice Summit. See also Robert Putnam and Nicholas Bayne, *Hanging Together – The Seven-Power Summits* (Cambridge, MA: Harvard University Press, 1984; revised and enlarged edition published by Sage, London, 1987).

14 See for example GATT, BISD 32 Supp. 44 (1986).

15 See 1955 OTC draft charter (*Final Act Adopted at the Ninth Session of the Contracting Parties*, Geneva, 1955, p. 183).

16 See Decision of 28 January 1987, GATT, BISD 33 Supp. 31, 34–5 (1987); GATT/1405, 5 February 1987.

17 See Jackson, Louis, and Matsushita, *Implementing the Tokyo Round*. See also Symposium on the Multilateral Trade Agreements II, *Law and Policy in International Business*, vol. 12 (1980), 1–334, in particular Jackson, 'The Birth of the GATT-MTN System: A Constitutional Appraisal', 21. See also McRae and Thames, 'The GATT and Multilateral Treaty Making: The Tokyo Round', *American Journal of International Law*, vol. 77 (1983) 51; and the contributions in *Cornell International Law Journal*, vol. 13 (1980), 145–290; and the MTN Studies commissioned by the Senate Finance Committee, 96th. Cong., 1st. Sess. (1979), (Comm. Prints 96–11 to 96–15).

18 See below, Chapter 6, especially 6.4.

19 The Arrangement Regarding Bovine Meat (GATT, BISD 26 Supp. 84 (1980)) and the International Dairy Arrangement (GATT, BISD 26 Supp. 91 (1980)) both have provisions referring to decision-making by consensus. The Agreement on the Implementation of Article VII (GATT, BISD 26 Supp. 116 (1980)) also has an explicit voting provision in Annexe II relating to the Technical Committee on Customs Valuation. The other MTN agreements do not explicitly refer to formal decision-making powers.

20 Jackson, *World Trade and the Law of GATT*, 74 et seq. See GATT, Article XXXIII.

21 Jackson, 'The Birth of the GATT-MTN System', above, note 17, at p. 40.

22 See Appendix.

23 See GATT Document GATT/LEG/1 and supplements.

24 The texts of the agreements and understanding can be found in GATT, BISD 26 Supp. (1980). See also Jackson, Louis, and Matsushita, *Implementing the Tokyo Round*.

25 See Robert Stern, John H. Jackson, and Bernard Hoekman, *An Assessment of the GATT Codes on Non-Tariff Measures* (Brookfield, VT: Gower, 1988). See also Jackson, 'The Birth of the GATT-MFN System', above, note 17.

26 The United States left the International Dairy Agreement at the end of 1984 after the EC had made sales of subsidized butter to the USSR (see *International Trade Reporter*, vol. 2 (1985) 12). Austria followed suit in March 1985 (*International Trade Reporter*, vol. 2 (1985), 429).

27 GATT, BISD 26 Supp. 201 (1980).

28 See especially the Declaration on Trade Measures Taken for Balance-of-Payments Purposes (GATT, BISD 26 Supp. 205 (1980)) and the Decision on Differential and More Favourable Treatment, Reciprocity and Fuller Participation of Developing Countries (GATT, BISD 26 Supp. 203 (1980)).

29 See Action by the Contracting Parties on the Multilateral Trade Negotiations (GATT, BISD 26 Supp. 201 (1980)).

30 See the 1969 Vienna Convention on the Law of Treaties, Article 31.

31 See above, Section 3.1 (a).

32 The United Kingdom accepted a number of Agreements on behalf of Hong Kong. On 23 April 1986 Hong Kong was deemed to be a member of the GATT in accordance with Article XXVI:5(c). Hong Kong, having declared its intentions to accept those Agreements, became a party thereto on that date. See GATT, *Status of Legal Instruments*, GATT/LEG/1, Chapter 16.

33 For example, Botswana which was not a member of GATT accepted the Customs Valuation Code. Similarly Bulgaria accepted the International Dairy Arrangement and the Bovine Meat Arrangement, and Guatemala signed the Bovine Meat Arrangement. Annexe IV, p. 172 to 'GATT Activities 1988'.

34 See Jackson, *World Trading System*, at p. 97.

35 See Francis G. Jacobs and Shelley Roberts (eds.), *The Effect of Treaties in Domestic Law* (London: Sweet and Maxwell, 1987).

36 Jackson, Louis, and Matsushita, *Implementing the Tokyo Round*, pp. 198–210.

37 Jackson and Davey, *Legal Problems of International Economic Relations*, at pp. 307–8.

38 Jackson, 'The General Agreement on Tariffs and Trade in United States Domestic Law', *Michigan Law Review*, vol. 66, (December 1967), p. 249.

39 See Jackson and Davey, *Legal Problems of International Economic Relations*, at pp. 79–84.

40 See Jackson, Louis, and Matsushita, *Implementing the Tokyo Round*, at p. 142.

41 The three basic treaties that establish the European Communities are the treaty establishing the European Coal and Steel Community (ECSC) (Treaty of Paris 1951); the treaty establishing the European Economic Community (EEC) (Treaty of Rome 1957); and the treaty establishing the European Atomic Energy Community (Euratom) (1957). The 1965 'Merger Treaty' established a single Council and Commission for the European Communities. Treaties of Accession were signed in 1972 with Denmark, Eire, and the UK, in 1980 with Greece, and in 1985 with Spain and Portugal. See Jackson 'United States–EEC Trade Relations: Constitutional Problems of Economic Interdependence', *Common Market Law Review*, vol. 16 (1979), 453. In 1987, the EC member states adopted an amending treaty called the 'Single European Act' which added to the constitutional structure of the EEC. See *Official Journal* L169, 29 June 1987, p. 1.

42 Article 113 of the EEC Treaty of Rome.

43 For example, Article 229 of the Treaty of Rome states that it shall be for the Commission to ensure the maintenance of appropriate relations with GATT. See also Jackson, Louis, and Matsushita, *Implementing the Tokyo Round*, Chapter 2.

44 See Jackson, Louis, and Matsushita, *Implementing the Tokyo Round*, at pp. 47–61; C.D. Ehlermann, 'Application of GATT Rules in the European Community', in Hilf, Jacobs, and Petersmann (eds.), *The European Community and GATT* (Deventer: Kluwer, 1986), pp. 187–249, at p. 201; Petersmann, 'Application of GATT by the Court of Justice of the European Communities', *Common Market Law Review*, vol. 20 (1983), 397–437.

45 See Chalmers Johnson, *MITI and the Japanese Miracle*, (Stanford: Stanford University Press, 1982), 47–9.

46 See Jackson, Louis, and Matsushita, *Implementing the Tokyo Round*, at Chapter 3.

47 Ibid. at p. 147.

Chapter 4

1 See GATT Document Press Release 1396, 25 September 1986, and BISD V. 33 at p. 19.

2 Jackson, *International Competition in Services.*

3 GATT Document GATT/1405 lists the decisions of January 1987 setting up the negotiating group structure, which includes the following:

Group on Negotiating Goods (GNG)
 Tariffs
 Non-Tariff Measures
 Natural Resource-Based Products
 Textiles and Clothing
 Agriculture
 Tropical Products
 GATT Articles
 MTN Agreements & Arrangements
 Safeguards
 Subsidies and Countervailing Measures
 Trade-Related Aspects of Intellectual Property Rights including Trade in Counterfeit Goods
 Trade-Related Investment Measures
 Dispute Settlement
 Functioning of the GATT System
Group of Negotiations on Services

4 See GATT Newsletter, No. 61, May 1989.

Chapter 5

1 The GATT panel reports ruling against the United States include: complainants Canada, EC, and Mexico against the United States, taxes on petroleum and certain imported substances (BISD V. 33, p. 136 (1987), and GATT Activities 1988, p. 92); complainants EC and Canada against the United States, import customs fee (GATT Activities 1987, p. 68); complainant EC against United States, Section 337 of the US Tariff Act of 1930 (GATT Activities 1988, p. 88); complainant Australia against US Sugar Quotas, BNA *International Trade Reporter*, vol. 6 (1989), p. 767. Processes in progress include one brought by Brazil against the United States regarding US trade action imposed because the United States argued that Brazil had given inadequate protection to intellectual property in the pharmaceutical area (GATT Activities 1988, p. 90). Another current process has been brought by the EC against the United States for US trade action in response to EEC restraints (alleged by the United States to be unfair or improper) on beef raised with the assistance of hormones.

2 See Louis Henkin, *How Nations Behave* (New York: Council on Foreign Relations, 2nd edn, 1979), 38–88.

3 Examples include the change of US law on DISC (Domestic International Sales Corporation). On reference to GATT, a compromise was reached between the parties leading to the rather vague and contradictory Council statement (GATT, BISD 28 Supp. 114 (1982)). In 1984 the US replaced the DISC system by the FSC system (26 USC §§921–7). See also the 1986 Customs Users' Fee case. During the congressional consideration of the 1986 Tax Reform Act, certain committees decided to impose a customs user's fee to add to tariffs at the border in order partially to fund the US Customs Service. The initial proposals were clearly contrary to GATT obligations. As a result of the criticisms of staff members of the committee, the proposals were redrafted so as to tie the amount of revenue raised to the total expenditure of the Customs Service. This would have allowed the US to claim that the measures were consistent with Article VIII of the GATT. However the provision was challenged and a GATT panel held the provisions were incompatible with GATT obligations (see *International Trade Reporter*, 4 (1987), 1450). Also in 1982, at the request of the European Community, a GATT Panel was established to consider the compatibility with the Agreement of the *US 'manufacturing clause'* (17 USC § 601). The Panel reported in May 1984 (GATT, BISD 31 Supp. 74 (1984)), concluding that the clause was inconsistent with Article XI and that its extension beyond 1 July 1982 was not compatible with US obligations. In 1986 a bill (S 1822 – HR 4696) was introduced which attempted to make the clause a permanent feature of US copyright law. In the hearings in the House, Ambassador Yeutter said:

> We have to be concerned about the fact that the manufacturing clause has been declared GATT illegal. Here we are attempting to strengthen the GATT, respond to the criticisms of the GATT that exist throughout the world, including in this subcommittee, appropriate criticisms in my judgment, but how do we go about reaching that objective, which all of us share, if we patently violate GATT ourselves.

> We have a definitive GATT decision against the United States on this clause. We have no defence whatsoever for the continuation of the manufacturing clause. How can we possibly go to other countries and say don't violate the GATT, if we cavalierly and flagrantly violate it ourselves.

(Hearing on HR 4696, House Ways and Means Committee, 99th Cong., 2nd Sess. (1986) 2). However the bill was not passed and the legislation lapsed.

4 See, e.g., Trimble, 'International Trade and the "Rule of Law"' *Michigan Law Review*, vol. 83 (1985), 1016.

5 See Jackson and Davey, *Legal Problems of International Economic Relations*, 273–6, 286–9; Henry Schermers, *International Institutional Law* (Rockville, MD: Sijthoff and Noordhoff, 2nd edn, 1980), 681–3.

6 See for example Robert Triffin, *The World Money Maze: National Currencies in International Payments* (New Haven, CT: Yale University Press, 1966).

7 Adapted from Jackson, 'Governmental Disputes in International Trade Relations', and Jackson, 'The Crumbling Institutions of the Liberal Trade System', *Journal of World Trade Law*, vol. 12 (1978), 98–101.

8 Robert Axelrod, *The Evolution of Cooperation* (New York: Basic Books, 1984).

9 Jan Tumlir, 'GATT Rules and Community Law', in Hilf, Jacobs, and Petersmann (eds.), *The European Community and GATT* (Deventer: Kluwer, 1986), pp. 6 and 20.

Chapter 6

1 Vienna Convention on the Law of Treaties, Article 32.

2 Annexe I, Notes and Supplementary Provisions. The *Basic Instruments* (Geneva: GATT/1969–7).

3 See above, Chapter 3.2.

4 See Ian Brownlie, *Principles of Public International Law* (Oxford: Clarendon Press, 3rd edn, 1979), pp. 21–3. Cf. E. McGovern, 'Dispute Settlement in the GATT – Adjudication or Negotiation?' in Hilf, Jacobs, and Petersmann (eds.), *The European Community and the GATT* (Deventer: Kluwer 1986), pp. 73–84.

5 Statute of the International Court of Justice, 59 Stat. 1055, T.S. 993. Article 59 reads: 'The decision of the Court has no binding force except between the parties and in respect of that particular case.'

6 See GATT, *Analytical Index*, Article I-12. See also Article I-15 (Chairman); Article I-16 (Chairman); Article II-20 (Secretariat).

7 Vienna Convention on the Law of Treaties, Article XXXI:3: 'There shall be taken into account, together with the context ... (b) any subsequent practice in the application of the treaty which establishes the agreement of the parties regarding its interpretation.'

8 See for example Articles of Agreement of the International Monetary Fund (60 Stat. 1401; TIAS 1501), Article XXIX, and Articles of Agreement of the International Bank for Reconstruction and Development (60 Stat. 1440; TIAS 1502), Article VIII.

9 See above, Chapter 2.1.

10 See below, note 44.

11 Havana (ITO) Charter Articles 92–7.

12 See Jackson, *World Trading System*, Section 4.2.

13 For texts of the 1979 MTN Agreements, see GATT, BISD 26 Supp. (1980).

14 See for example the Agreement on Implementation of Article VII of the GATT (GATT, BISD 26 Supp. 116 (1980), Article 20:5).

15 See for example the Agreement on Government Procurement (GATT, BISD 26 Supp. 33 (1980) Article VII:9).

16 See works by Jackson in the Select Bibliography, and also McGovern, above, note 4.

17 Oliver Long (former Director-General of GATT), *Law and its Limitations in the GATT Multilateral Trade System* (Boston: Kluwer, 1985) 73, citing Dam, *The GATT*, 356.

18 Arthur Dunkel, Director-General of GATT, as reported in GATT/1312, 5 March 1982.

19 See Long, above, note 17, at p. 21: 'GATT is at the same time a legal framework and a forum for negotiation'. See also Hudec, 'GATT or GABB?', *Yale Law Journal*, vol. 80 (1971), 1299.

20 Statement of Harry Hawkins, representing the US, speaking about the proposed ITO charter at the London meeting of the Preparatory Committee of the United Nations Conference on Trade and Employment, UN Doc. EPCT/C.II/PV.2, 8 (1946).

21 See charter of the ITO, Chapter VIII, Articles 92–7, UN, Final Act and Related Documents, UN Conference on Trade and Employment, held at Havana, Cuba, from 21 November 1947 to 24 March 1948, Interim Commission for the International Trade Organization, Lake Success, New York, April 1948. UN Doc. E/Conf. 2/78. See also Clair Wilcox, *A Charter for World Trade* (New York: Macmillan, 1949), 159, 305–308.

22 See Wilcox, above, note 21, at p. 159.

23 Ibid. at p. 160.

24 GATT, BISD 14 Supp. 18 (1967).

25 GATT, BISD 11 Supp. 95 (1963).

26 Generally on the GATT dispute settlement procedure, see Davey, 'Dispute-settlement in GATT', *Fordham International Law Journal*, vol. 11 (1987), 51; Plank, 'An Unofficial Description of How a GATT Panel Works and Does Not' *Swiss Review of International Competition Law*, vol. 29 (1987), 81; McGovern, above, note 4.

27 Jackson, *World Trade and the Law of GATT*, pp. 164ff.

28 GATT Article XXIII. An action may also be brought under Article XXIII when the attainment of any objective of the Agreement is being impeded.

29 The Australian ammonium sulphate case, GATT, BISD Vol. II, 188 (1952). See Hudec, 'Retaliation Against Unreasonable Foreign Trade

Practices', *Minnesota Law Review*, vol. 59 (1975) 46; Hudec, *GATT Legal System*, 144–53.

30 The Australian ammonium sulphate case (above, note 29) and the German sardines case (GATT, BISD 1 Supp. 53 (1953)) both endorsed the view that the GATT should be construed to protect 'reasonable expectations' of the contracting parties. See Hudec, *GATT Legal System*, 144–53, and Hudec, 'GATT or GABB?' above, note 19, 1341.

31 GATT, BISD 3 Supp. 224 (1955).

32 GATT Doc. L/1222/Add. 1 (1960). See also Jackson, *World Trade and the Law of GATT*, at p. 182.

33 United States Taxes on Petroleum and certain imported substances, Report of Panel adopted 17 June 1987, GATT Doc. BISD V. 34, p. 136 (L/6175).

34 See Hudec, *GATT Legal System*, 66–96.

35 Some of this information was obtained from private conversations with senior GATT officials closely associated with the early development of GATT.

36 Understanding Regarding Notification, Consultation, Dispute Settlement and Surveillance, GATT, BISD 26 Supp. 210 (1980), especially paragraphs 10–21.

37 Netherlands Measures of Suspension of Obligations to the United States, GATT, BISD 1 Supp. 32 (1953). This was one result of the US Congress's enactment of Section 22 of the Agriculture Act in 1951. See Jackson and Davey, *Legal Problems of International Economic Relations*, at p. 956. The Netherlands never enforced the quota, arguably because of its ineffectiveness in removing the US quota on dairy products. See Hudec, 'Retaliation Against Unreasonable Foreign Trade Practices' above, note 29, at p. 57.

38 As a result of the panel decision in the oil tax case (GATT, BISD 34 Supp. 136 (1988); see below, note 39), the EC requested that the CONTRACTING PARTIES authorize retaliation (*International Trade Reporter*, vol. 5 (1988), 681 and 1303–4).

39 For example in the citrus case, as a result of the failure of the EC to accept the findings of a 1985 GATT panel (*International Trade Reporter*, vol. 2 (1985), 162), the US President authorized retaliatory measures against imports of EC pasta (Proclamation 5354 of 21 June 1985, *Federal Register*, vol. 50 (1985), 26143). However, in the light of continuing discussion between the EC and US, the President issued Proclamation 5363 of 15 August 1985 (*Federal Register*, vol. 50 (1985), 33711) suspending the application of the duty until 1 November 1985. The duties remained in force until 21 August 1986 when the President revoked the increased rates of duty due to a settlement of the citrus case (*Federal Register*, vol. 51 (1986), 30146). However it

115

must be noted that trade in pasta between the US and EC was itself a problem, and so retaliation against a problematic product may have had a certain added attraction.

40 See above, note 36.

41 See GATT Newsletter, No. 61, May 1989.

42 The increase in cases was due partly to a decision by the US to utilize the GATT dispute settlement processes more fully, and partly to the 1974 US Trade Act, Section 301, which established a presumption that cases initiated under Section 301 procedures would be taken to GATT when appropriate.

43 Much of the specific information and statistics about GATT disputes contained in this section are derived from a study I have made, based on an inventory of GATT disputes developed over a number of years and contained in a computer database. See Jackson, *World Trading System*, Chapter 4.4.

44 On compliance with ICJ rulings, see Weissberg, 'Role of the International Court of Justice in the UN System: the First Quarter-Century', in Dobbs Ferry, *The Future of the International Court of Justice* (New York: Oceana, 1976), 137–50, 170–74.

45 See above, note 43.

46 See Brownlie, above, note 4, 495–505.

47 Trade Expansion Act of 1962, §252, Pub.L. 87–794, 76 Stat. 872.

48 Fisher and Steinhardt, 'Section 301 of the Trade Act of 1974: Protection for US Exporters of Goods, Services, and Capital', *Law and Policy in International Business*, vol. 14 (1982), 569.

49 The enactment of the 1988 Omnibus Act met with a great deal of criticism from foreign nations, particularly the EC and Japan. The EC protested against the passing of the Act at the September GATT Council meeting (*International Trade Reporter*, vol. 5 (1988), 1302) and on 26 September 1988 the EC Council of Ministers released a statement expressing 'serious concern' over the Act (*European Community News*, No. 24/88). Japanese officials also expressed concern over the Act: see *Financial Times*, 5 August 1988, and *Wall Street Journal*, 4 August 1988.

50 Trade Act of 1974 (as amended to December 1988), sections 301–306, 19 USCA §§2411–2416 (1980 and Supp 1988). As to application to services, see 19 USCA §2411(e)(1)(A) (1980 and Supp. 1988).

51 The legislative history of the 1974 Act made it clear that the President was not obliged to refer a section 301 action to the GATT; see Comm. Rpt. No. 93–1298, Senate Finance Committee, 93rd Cong. 2nd Sess. (1974), reprinted in *US Code Congressional and Administrative News*, vol. 4 (1974), 7186, 7304. However the Trade Agreements Act of 1979 (§901, 93 Stat. 295, 19 USCA §§2413–2414 (1980 and

Supp. 1988)) introduced a new section, section 303, which requires that the USTR refer the matter to international dispute settlement procedures where applicable. It is clear that the dispute settlement procedure need not be fully completed before the USTR can recommend action.

52 19 USCA §2411(e)(3) (1980 and Supp. 1988). See Hansen, 'Defining Unreasonableness in International Trade: Section 301 of the Trade Act of 1974', *Yale Law Journal*, vol. 96 (1987), 1122.

53 19 USCA §2411(a)(1)(B)(ii) (1980 and Supp. 1988).

54 For legislative history of the original 1974 Act, see *US Code Congressional and Administrative News*, vol. 4 (1974), 7186.

55 See, e.g., US actions against Brazil because of US arguments that Brazil failed to provide adequate protection for intellectual property for pharmaceutical products, and US actions against the EC for reasons of EC restrictions on beef produced using hormones, GATT Activities 1988, pp. 90 and 72.

56 Council Regulation (EEC) 2641/84, OJ [1984] L.252/1.

57 See Eric Stein, Peter Hay, and Michel Waelbroeck, *European Community Law and Institutions in Perspective: Text, Cases and Readings* (Indianapolis: Bobbs Merrill, 1976) (with Supplement) (1985), 66 et seq.

58 Article 13 of Regulation 2641/84.

59 M.C.E.J. Bronckers, *Selected Safeguard Measures in Multilateral Trade Relations* (Deventer: Kluwer, 1985), 210. Cf. Bourgeois and Laurent, 'Le "Nouvel Instrument de Politique Commerciale": Un Pas en Avant Vers l'Elimination des Obstacles aux Echanges Internationaux', *Revue Trimestrielle de Droit Européen*, vol. 21 (1985), 41.

60 Two early cases were formally initiated under the EEC Regulation. The first, between the Dutch company Akzo and the US company DuPont, concerned aramid fibres (Notice of Initiation, OJ [1986] C.25/2; Commission Decision to refer to GATT, OJ [1987] L.117/18). A GATT panel ruled against the United States. The second dealt with intellectual property protection in Indonesia, and the result was a change in Indonesian policy with respect to enforcement of intellectual property rights (Notice of Initiation, OJ [1987] C.136/3; Notice of Suspension of Procedure, OJ [1987] L.335/22; and Termination of Procedure following undertaking by Indonesian Government, OJ [1988] L.123/51).

61 See Statements of Ambassador Yeutter, S.Hrg. 99–216, Senate Committee on Finance, 99th Cong., 1st Sess., 12–89; Statement of Ambassador Yeutter, Com. Ser. 99–96, House Ways and Means Committee, 99th Cong., 2nd Sess., 3–40.

62 See Jackson, 'Governmental Disputes in International Trade Relations', pp. 8–13.

63 Ibid., pp. 15–16; see also Jackson, 'MTN and the Legal Institutions of International Trade, MTN Studies', Comm. Print 96–14, 96th Cong., 1st Sess., 17 (1979).

64 Article 38, Statute of the International Court of Justice, 59 Stat. 1055, T.S. 993.

65 See for example the US-Canada Free Trade Agreement, *International Legal Materials*, vol. XXVII (1988), 281.
The dispute settlement provisions of the US-Canada Free Trade Agreement contain two distinct tracks. The first, found in Chapter 18, deals with general problems relating to the Agreement, the second (Chapter 19) with more specific problems arising under anti-dumping or countervailing duty provisions.
These provisions have been seen by some as a potential model for dispute settlement in the Uruguay Round; see for example *Congressional Record*, vol. 134 (1988), H6626 (statement of Mr. Crane) and H6640 (statement of Mr. Bereuter).

66 Ibid., Article 1904. On the US side the implementation of this provision was carried out by section 401(c)(g)(7) of the United States-Canada Free Trade Implementation Act of 1988, Pub. L. 100–449; 102 Stat.

67 Jackson, Louis, and Matsushita, *Implementing the Tokyo Round*, 208–209.

68 Giorgio Malinverni, *Le Règlement des Différends dans les Organisations Internationales Economiques* (Leiden: Sijthoff, 1974), 106, quoted in Long, above, note 17, at p. 7.

69 See above, notes 17 and 26.

70 GATT, BISD 18 Supp. 149, 158, 166 (1970–71); 19 Supp. 97 (1972); 20 Supp. 145–209 (1973).

71 See GATT Document Press Release 1396, 25 September 1986 and BISD V. 33 at p.19; also GATT Newsletter, No. 61, May 1989.

72 See GATT, *Review of Developments in the Trading System*, a biannual survey of developments affecting international trade, issued by the GATT Secretariat.

73 GATT Newsletter, No. 61, May 1989 and No. 64, August-September 1989.

Chapter 7

1 The following GATT CPs are often considered 'non-market' or 'state-trading':

Cuba
Czechoslovakia
Hungary
Poland
Romania
Yugoslavia.
See Patterson, 'Improving GATT Rules for Non-Market Economies', *Journal of World Trade Law*, vol. 20 (1986), 185. See also Ianni, 'The International Treatment of State Trading', *Journal of World Trade Law*, vol. 18 (1982), 480; and Grzybowski, 'Socialist Countries in GATT', *American Journal of Comparative Law*, vol. 28 (1980), 539.
3 Jackson, *World Trading System*, p. 295, and Chapters 10 and 11.

Chapter 8

1 See Capotorti, Hilf, Jacobs, and Jacque, *The European Union Treaty: Commentary on the Draft adopted by the European Parliament on 14 February 1984* (Oxford: Clarendon Press, 1986).
2 See American Law Institute, *Annual Reports* (Philadelphia: 1989), especially p. 83ff, and *The National Conference of Commissions on Uniform State Laws, 1987–88 Reference Book*, published by the Conference (Chicago: 1988).
3 See, e.g., Jackson, *International Competition in Services*.
4 See Jackson, 'Governmental Disputes in International Trade Relations', pp. 8–13.
5 See above, note 3.
6 See the negotiating objectives concerning intellectual property in GATT Document Press Release 1396, 25 September 1986 and BISD V. 33 at p. 19; also GATT Newsletter, No. 61, May 1989.
7 Interim Commission for the ITO, established in 1948 and still the legal entity for certain GATT purposes. See Jackson, *World Trade and the Law of GATT*, at Chapters 2 and 6.
8 Jackson, *World Trading System*, at p. 95. See also Jackson, *Governmental Disputes in International Trade Relations*.
9 Lindley H. Clark, Jr., 'Our Do-It-Yourself Trade Policy', *Wall Street Journal*, 22 September 1989, p. A10.

SELECT BIBLIOGRAPHY

Other works by John H. Jackson relating to this subject include:

World Trade and the Law of GATT (Indianapolis: Bobbs-Merrill Company, December 1969). Treatise on a Legal Analysis of the General Agreement on Tariffs and Trade.

Legal Problems of International Economic Relations (St Paul: West Publishing Company, August 1977). Cases, Materials and Text on the National and International Regulation of International Economic Relations. Approximately 1100 pages plus Document Supplement. *Second Edition* co-authored with Professor William J. Davey (West Publishing Company, August 1986).

Implementing the Tokyo Round: National Constitutions and International Economic Rules (Ann Arbor: University of Michigan Press, June 1984). Co-authored with Professor Jean-Victor Louis (Belgium) and Professor Mitsuo Matsushita (Japan).

International Trade Policy: The Lawyer's Perspective (New York: Matthew Bender, 1985). Symposium co-edited with Richard O. Cunningham and Claude G.B. Fontheim. Produced through the Committee on International Trade, Section of International Law and Practice, of the American Bar Association.

International Competition in Services: A Constitutional Framework (American Enterprise Institute for Public Policy Research, Washington DC, 1988).

The World Trading System: Law and Policy of International Economic Relations (Cambridge MA: MIT Press, 1989).

120

Anti-Dumping Law & Practice: A Comparative Study (Ann Arbor: University of Michigan Press, 1989). Co-authored with Edwin A. Vermulst, Belgium.

'Governmental Disputes in International Trade Relations: A Proposal in the Context of GATT', *Journal of World Trade Law*, vol. 13 (January-February 1979), no. 1.

Readers may also be interested in the following:

The GATT Legal System and World Trade Diplomacy by Robert Hudec (New York: Praeger, 1975).

The GATT: Law and International Economic Organization by Kenneth Dam (Chicago: University of Chicago Press, 1970).

International Trade Regulation by Edmond McGovern (Exeter: Globefield Press, 2nd edn, 1986).

Multilateral Commercial Diplomacy by Gerard Curzon (London: Michael Joseph, 1965).

GATT, droit international et commerce mondial by Thiebaut Flory (Paris: Librairie Générale du Droit et Jurisprudence, 1968).

The European Community and GATT eds. Meinhard Hilf, Francis Jacobs, and Ernst-Ulrich Petersmann (Deventer: Kluwer, 1986).

The Case for a New Global Trade Organization by Miriam Camps (New York: Council on Foreign Relations, 1980).

The American Challenge for World Trade – US Interests in the GATT Multilateral Trading System by Ernest H. Preeg (Washington: Center for Strategic and International Studies, 1985).

CHATHAM HOUSE PAPERS

General Series Editor: William Wallace
Programme Director: J.M.C. Rollo

The Royal Institute of International Affairs, at Chatham House in London, has provided an impartial forum for discussion and debate on current international issues for 70 years. Its resident research fellows, specialized information resources, and range of publications, conferences, and meetings span the fields of international politics, economics, and security. The Institute is independent of government.

Chatham House Papers are short monographs on current policy problems which have been commissioned by the RIIA. In preparing the papers, authors are advised by a study group of experts convened by the RIIA, and publication of a paper indicates that the Institute regards it as an authoritative contribution to the public debate. The Institute does not, however, hold opinions of its own; the views expressed in this publication are the responsibility of the author.

ACKNOWLEDGEMENTS

I have benefited from the advice of many persons, including the members of an advisory group established by the Royal Institute of International Affairs at Chatham House. I particularly want to acknowledge the assistance of Francis Jacobs, Dr DeAnne Julius of Chatham House, and Dr Phedon Nicolaides of Chatham House. Needless to say, however, the views expressed in this manuscript are entirely my own.

October 1989   John H. Jackson